Miss Elizabeth

Miss Elizabeth

A Memoir

by

Elizabeth Anderson *and* Gerald R. Kelly

Boston   **LITTLE, BROWN AND COMPANY**   *Toronto*

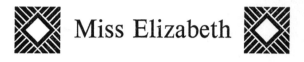 Miss Elizabeth

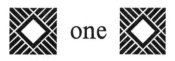 one

I was born in 1884 in Saginaw, Michigan, a small town of about sixty thousand citizens. The Saginaw River ran through the center of town, conveniently creating the social division that existed in most small towns of that time. On the west side of the river were the aristocrats and on the east side, where my family lived, were the people who did the business and kept things moving along in Saginaw.

The town had been settled mostly by Germans who were solid people with both-feet-squarely-on-the-ground. They were mildly astonished by the Prall family, particularly by my mother, who had come there from the West Indies and was European both in taste and ancestry. She smoked cigarettes openly at a time when even men who smoked "coffin nails" were considered decadent. A woman who smoked was obviously fallen. When it became generally known that wine was a regular part of our meals and that I, my brother David, and my sisters, Dorothea and Margaret, were allowed to drink it, most of the townspeople concluded that we were rapidly going to the dogs.

Fortunately, the people who knew us well found it in their hearts to forgive us these transgressions. My mother was a good and a kind woman who liked to garden and that made up for a multitude of "differences." My father was a prosperous businessman who owned a chain of three drugstores and was respectable in most other ways. If we smoked and drank red wine and if our house sometimes rang with loud laughter and talk, it was something that the neighbors managed to live with.

My father went on occasional excursions to Chicago where he had an interest in a factory that made soda fountains, and these were exciting times for the whole family. We knew he would return on the midnight train and all of us would troop down to the station to meet him. Most of Saginaw would be respectably in bed at that hour, but the Prall family would be lined up on the station platform, waiting. Then the steam engine would chug and sputter to a halt, enveloping us briefly in a great wreath of steam, and my father would appear; laughing and already talking and always carrying a huge box of the most indigestible food he could find in Chicago. We would return home then, and open the package — sometimes a fantastic array of chocolates. Mother would bring out her freshly baked mince pies and Father would pass around glasses of beer. We would stay up until the early hours of the morning, shouting with laughter at the exaggerated stories of his hectic time in Chicago.

As soon as I was able to walk around on my own, Mother whisked me off on an unexpected trip to the West Indies. I was the oldest of her children and she felt obliged to show me off to her family there. By that time I had heard all about how I happened to have some relatives in the West Indies and how they had come to Michigan.

When my grandmother was a young girl of fifteen in England, her mother had been dead for some time. Her father was an invalid and seemed to feel he was ill-equipped to raise two daughters. He called my grandmother into his room one day and, in his very elegant, old-fashioned English, asked, "Mary, would you like to be married? Mr. Dier has proposed for your hand."

My grandmother thought about it and about her

sister who was two years older and said, "Well, I do think it would be fun to get married before sister Anna."

So the child of fifteen was promptly married off to an old roué from the West Indies and they sailed off to Antigua together. Like all bachelors in the Islands, Mr. Dier had a mulatto mistress and she turned out to be disgruntled at the unexpected appearance of a young English rival who set about running the household and otherwise poaching on her preserves. The mulatto girl was so outraged by the situation that she tried to poison my grandmother and very nearly succeeded in killing her. For weeks my grandmother was wracked with cramps, and from that time on her little body servant, Sophia, had to taste every bit of food before she ate it. At that time and in that place, no one seemed much concerned about what might happen to the little Negro girl.

My grandfather later sailed with his family to Canada and kept on going until he reached Michigan, so that when Mother took me to the West Indies, there was only my great-aunt, Sophronisba Isabel, to visit.

Sophronisba lived alone except for her servants in a huge old white house my grandfather had built. It was made of stucco and stone and arranged in the Spanish style, around an open court. I was greatly impressed by the house and somewhat frightened, too. It was not like any of the houses I had ever seen before.

Great-aunt Sophronisba did not rush out to greet us, though she had the servants install us comfortably in a separate section of the house. She was a chronic hypochondriac and remained in her bed most of the time. She was so old that she had given up inventing new diseases to suffer from and was simply "poorly" and "abed." An ancient nurse with a resolute, bulldog face came to our rooms and told Mother she was going to take me on the requisite courtesy call to Great-aunt Sophronisba Isabel. Mother plucked a rose from a nearby vase and told me to present it to the resident head of the family.

The old nurse and I went through a long series of rooms, all hung with cotton curtains that had been soaked in carbolic acid, and with each step I was growing more terrified because of the cloying, oppressive smell and the ancient mustiness of the dreary rooms. It seemed like miles to me and I was hanging back fearfully by the time we reached the master bedroom of Great-aunt Sophronisba Isabel.

She was propped up in a huge canopied bed with a huge, oddly frivolous, frilled nightcap on her wizened gray head. I cringed before the stern old creature who was the oldest human being I had ever seen. A miasma of carbolic acid hovered about her as she glared down at me.

The nurse said: "Here is Janey's child. Janey's little girl."

I timidly held the rose out to her and she frowned at it suspiciously for a long time. Finally she snapped, "Has that thing been fumigated?"

I dropped the rose and fled from the room instantly, leaving the nurse and the great-aunt far behind me. I was quite sure I had not been fumigated and I was determined not to have it done to me.

Mother did not inflict many more such experiences on me, and in a short time we returned to the United States and to the warm, comforting stability of Saginaw.

We had moved, by then, to a larger house on the edge of town and it was surrounded by fine, beautiful elm trees. Mother was finally able to fully indulge her passion for gardening, even to the extent of hiring a funny, fussy old gardener named Atherton. Father always called him *Mrs.* Atherton, but he and Mother grew asters such as I have never seen anywhere else. They planted the flowers so close together that when they bloomed there were great stretches of rich color around the house. All the asters seemed to come out at the same time, suddenly bursting into a fire of purple, pink, white and blue.

For some reason of her own, Mother planted parsley, of all things, along the driveway in front of the house. It was a cheerful, bright green complement to the asters and I liked the idea very much, but there was a strong taste of parsley to almost everything we ate.

I was happy to be home again, back from the Indies which had been strange and unsettling for me. I spent my days cultivating friendships with the squirrels that came to the balcony outside my room. They came to trust me so completely that they would jump into the room and sit on the floor, eating the nuts I had scattered about.

Saginaw was a good place to grow up in, with woods for wandering and rivers for roaming. People were friendly and unaffected and pleasures were simple. There were, to be sure, certain drawbacks, but they did not seem important to me. The springs around Saginaw were not good and the river water was contaminated, so the drinking water had to be hauled in by enormous trucks from Bay City, twenty miles away.

There was another unfortunate aspect to the area, one that grew steadily worse as time went on. All the farmers near Saginaw unaccountably began to grow beets to be made into sugar. The sugar beets were pressed and the remains were simply thrown onto the ground and forgotten. After a time, they could no longer be forgotten nor forgiven. When the wind was blowing from a certain direction, it was an ill wind indeed, for the air smelled unbearably like garbage. Finally the local powers had to call a halt to the casual, carefree disposal of beet sugar refuse and the air gradually lost its pungency.

As a child, I was ill a good part of the time and I rarely went to school for a full year. Instead, I remained at home, studying sometime, reading most of the time, and generally devising my own diversions.

I was fascinated by all the colorful, eccentric old men who ambled about the city or drove around in carriages. They were mostly lumbermen who had grown rich cutting down all the trees for miles around and were now retired, with nothing to do but keep a wary eye on each other and the town in general. Many of them would come each day to my father's largest drugstore and would sit around exchanging gossip and recounting hoary tales of the proud past. I always loved to find some discreetly obscure place to sit and listen to the talk of who had died and who might, and to the sometimes lurid stories about the boisterous logging days.

One of the regulars was old Mr. Burt, who was a millionaire, people said. They also said he was so crotchety and cross that no one could bear to be around him for long. Each day at an unvarying hour he would drive up to the drugstore in his little sulky, with his dog sitting at his side. He left the dog in the buggy all morning, with the reins carefully arranged over his head.

Three times a week, at precisely five o'clock in the afternoon, a very wealthy old lady would drive up to our house to have tea with my mother, who was probably the only person in town who served it. She rode about in an elegant electric automobile with a steering stick and a black-cushioned interior decorated with silken tassels. She had gotten it into her head that I was a "good, sound, no-nonsense child," and every Saturday she would ask me to have her automobile recharged. Driving the car, even for a short distance, was always the highlight of my week.

When I was old enough to have learned to operate a typewriter, Father asked me to type his business letters for him. I was not an expert stenographer, but I usually knew what Father was trying to say and the letters somehow came out all right. The job had little pay but certain rewarding dividends, for Father began taking me along on his periodic trips to Chicago.

The business excuse that we had agreed upon was that I would accompany him as his secretary. We stayed in the wonderful old hotels of that era and I was dizzy with the new sights and sounds and smells that seemed to hurl themselves at my senses.

I caught shocking glimpses from afar of impossibly lush nudes hanging over the bar in taverns that were forbidden to women. I sat, nearly lost, in huge overstuffed chairs in the bustling, glamorous lobby, waiting for Father to appear and expose me to some new adventure.

Most of my dining was done alone, however, for Father favored various clubs where an eighteen-year-old girl would not be welcomed. But I enjoyed this too, sitting in solitary splendor in a elegant restaurant, with glittering crystal glasses and gleaming silver. I would haughtily scan the menu, looking for at least one dish I was familiar with and could pronounce.

We would return in high style on the train and be greeted, as always, by the rest of the family. The late night sessions of eating and talking would be enlivened by my own contribution to the tales of big city life.

I missed the Chicago trips after I enrolled in the University of Michigan, but new dimensions were added to my life, both by the university and the city of Ann Arbor. I met people my own age who were interested in the books and music I had always enjoyed and who talked about such things with spirit and animation. The university was coeducational and, indeed, had been one of the first colleges to admit women as students, but in those days the usual contact between the sexes was in the meeting of minds. Male students led separate existences in rigidly separated dormitories and females were generally left to entertain themselves, often by pairing off and riding in sulkies about the lovely paths and lanes near the Huron River, which ran through Ann Arbor. It was here that I acquired a lasting love for horses, and I was one of the daring few who rode other than sidesaddle.

Ann Arbor was the trade center of Washtenaw County, a rich farming and fruit-growing area. In the fall harvest time, the town was besieged by wagons and trucks and flat-bottomed boats as the farmers brought their produce, like offerings, to the markets. I would walk for hours in the market, marveling at the rich smells and varied sights, the hectic atmosphere of buying and selling.

At the university I majored in Latin and Greek and found that I enjoyed the quiet life of the scholar. My Latin professor was a tall, angular man who wore steel-rimmed spectacles and who would wander absently about the room as he lectured. He had a penchant for identifying students by other means than proper names, so that one might be called "Mr. Sports" if he were an athlete, and another might be, to him, "Miss Blue Notebook." He had somehow learned where I came from and quite often I would hear him say something like, "This morning we will hear declensions by Miss Saginaw." I never minded, but often wondered by what odd process Saginaw became more memorable than Prall.

The time I spent in the University of Michigan was unmarked by memorable event. I lived close enough to return often to Saginaw, where I could display bright fragments of my new education to a loving family, who never seemed to mind. Such reunions were always occasions for parties, even though they were likely to occur each weekend, and my recollections of my family during that period are those of happy gatherings and fine, festive times.

After I was graduated from the University of Michigan, I began looking around for a job and found one in Humboldt, a little mining village in upper Michigan. They needed a teacher at the small high school there, I was told when I was offered the position.

I had no idea what I was getting myself into. I thought I had been hired to teach Latin and English, but it turned out that I was also required to teach Roman history and German, and when the superintendent and the principal took a few weeks off to go hunting, which was often, I taught all the rest of the subjects as well.

When I stepped off the train in Humboldt, I was

appalled. I had not expected to find a town quite so tiny, quite so crude. The miners lived in little huts scattered all over the place, and the only hotel was a wooden structure with paper-thin walls. Whatever went on in any part of the hotel was instantly known in all other parts. The school proved to be a square, ugly building in the center of town and all of the miners' many children attended it.

I settled into the hotel and set about teaching with firm resolution. It was unthinkable that I should fail at my first job. I was surprised and pleased to find that it was not as formidable a task as I had feared. For some reason, I got along well with the children and subsequently with their parents. It must have been a matter of natural chemistry, for the townspeople also took inexplicable dislikes to certain people and let it be known in many emphatic ways. That had happened to the last teacher, I was told.

Humboldt had a sprinkling of all the tides of immigration to the United States. There were Welshmen, Germans, Italians, Irish and Poles, all living in their own groups. There were little ethnic celebrations going on all the time and it gave Humboldt a festive air that had not existed in Saginaw. There seemed to be thousands of children running freely in the streets, but I later decided that it was only because they ran so swiftly and shouted so loudly that they seemed so numerous. There could only have been hundreds.

Winter came on, fierce and cold and, in its way, quite wonderful. Deep snows drifted where the wind willed it and even the simple act of going from the hotel to the school became an adventure. Everyone had to be bundled and rebundled against any possible invasion of the bitter winds; walking was a matter of carefully balancing one's way along narrow paths in the snow, made by others who had gone before. Noses, cheeks and ears glowed cherry red and steam trailed from mouths, looking like individual clouds.

Some of the more ambitious boys of the town had gone off to mining college and they returned for the holidays. Their sisters and I were invited — dared, really — to join them on a nearby lake for an afternoon of iceboating. I had not done anything like that before and had to be shown where to sit and how to handle the rudder and how to tack.

The iceboats were only big enough to hold one person at a time, and when it was my turn, I tightly clutched the ropes attached to the front rudder. Then the wind billowed the sail and the boat began to skim along the surface of the ice, slowly at first, then picking up to a reckless speed. I was fully aware that the hard cold ice was only inches below me and that I was moving faster than I ever had before. I held the rudder steady, afraid to turn, and then, as the shore of the lake came closer, afraid not to turn. I eased off to the right and almost instantly, it seemed, the boom jerked over my head and the sailboat soared around in a circle that would return me, more or less, to my starting point. It was a terrifying, yet exhilarating experience, and we kept at it long after we were numb with cold and breathless with exhaustion.

Later in the winter there was a particularly bad blizzard, one that stalled the train not far from Humboldt. All the passengers climbed out of the train and trudged through the swirling snow to the hotel. This was nothing new. Trains were stopped by the snow quite often and the passengers would suddenly appear at the hotel, clamoring for food and lodging.

During this storm, however, the cook suddenly decided she was being overworked. She and her daughter had been doing all the cooking and cleaning at the hotel and she had finally reached her limit. She stopped her work, quit her job, and marched out into the worst storm of the year.

I was in my room, preparing to go down to dinner, when the owner of the hotel came up and told me that there would be no dinner that night for anyone. I listened to his troubles with a sympathetic ear and finally offered to lend a hand in the kitchen.

He accepted my offer so quickly that I concluded he had expected it all along. I ended up by doing all the cooking for three days, and I was excused from teaching school for that time. I had nearly reached the point of following the previous cook's precedent when the rail was cleared and someone was sent in from another city to take over the cooking.

In the spring, the surging beauty of the countryside emerged with the green foliage and wild flowers. I would be seized with sudden intense desires to go hunting for wintergreen or arbutus, which creeps along close to the ground, with the pinkness of the flowers barely visible under the leaves.

Humboldt began to look much better to me, in its physical aspects at least, but there was still a stifling lack of companionship. There was simply no one around to talk to.

I was beginning to feel the pangs of solitude when the pangs of a sudden attack of appendicitis took the matter out of my hands. Humboldt had a doctor for the miners, of course, but he was unequipped or unwilling to operate on me. I recovered somewhat from the attack but the same doctor insisted that I go home to be treated properly.

In Saginaw, our family physician decided to operate and I went into the hospital to be looked after by the Sisters of St. Vincent de Paul. They wore enormous coifs of starched white linen and blue woolen habits, and around their necks they had massive wooden rosaries which I was certain weighed at least thirty pounds.

When I had recuperated from the operation, I took a job in a high school as a substitute teacher in education. I knew nothing at all about the subject, but the teacher who was leaving gave me a few tips on "How to Tell Stories to Children" which I passed along to the students, and I improvised a few suggestions of my own. In those days, people were not as concerned about the qualifications of a teacher. If she were a nice person who got on well with the pupils it seemed to work out just as well.

At that same time I did a great deal of strolling around, thinking and wondering what I would do with my life when this temporary job was over. My father was quick to notice my preoccupation and he talked to me about my future.

He suggested that I should go somewhere and do something different and finally asked: "What would you like to do?"

But that was the question that had been plaguing me. I hesitated a long time before answering. My sisters and I were always reluctant to tell Father what we wanted to do because we knew he would encourage us to do it, even if it had been only an idle daydream.

Finally Father said, "Why don't you try New York, honey?"

The idea was no stranger to me. I had been working it over in my mind for some time. "Well, it would be kind of interesting to go to a library school there, if that agrees with you," I said, and it was settled.

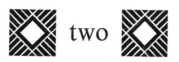 two

New York was, for me, what later came to be called a "cultural shock." Too much has already been written about First Impressions of the Big City, but I had them all. For days I hovered close to the hotel I had checked into, then decided I would be able to find my way to the library school, which was in the main branch of the New York Public Library.

I was awed by the people on Fifth Avenue. They were walking so rapidly and so determinedly that it was obvious they knew exactly where they were going. I was not even quite sure where I was.

Then I came to the library, that imposing, handsome structure guarded by two benign, concrete lions. For some minutes I stood looking up at the building, oblivious to the small island I had created in the river of pedestrians simply by standing still while people flowed by me on either side.

Finally I climbed the steps, noting the number of readers and loungers and lunch eaters sitting there. Here, at least, were people who seemed to have no place to go and did not mind at all.

At the information desk inside, I asked for a Miss Plummer of the Library School and was directed downstairs, through a maze of corridors and stairwells.

Miss Plummer was a wonderful woman of great dignity and great warmth. Quite efficiently she settled me into the school, found me a place to live, and told me how to travel to and from both places.

The Library School took up a vast amount of space in the basement of the library, stretching out over great expanses of cold stone floor. It seemed constantly to be hurrying from one place to another, stopping only for classes and random lectures. I did well enough at the school to be given a job at the library when I had completed the requisite courses. I came to know the library in all its complex and intimate details as I went about locating the books to be used to teach cataloguing. I moved on to other jobs later, steadily learning more about the operation of the library, which is at least as complicated as that of a large hotel.

For a time I lived in a "railroad flat" on 110th Street. The rooms were strung out like beads and it was necessary to pass through every room in the place to reach the kitchen at the back. I shared the apartment with an older woman who had recently come from Germany. She was friendly enough but seemed to brood with sullen intensity about the fate and future of her native land. She kept telling me what an easy life Americans had, and she had so many minor prejudices that she was difficult to live with. I never knew when I might tread on a tender bias and set her to complaining again.

The neighborhood around East 110th Street was littered and run-down, verging on a slum but never quite becoming one. One night I stayed too late at a party at the school and had to return home alone on the El. When I got off at my stop, shops were closed and shuttered and the street was eerie and deserted. For the party I had worn a flowery summer dress and a large picture hat and I was very much out of place in that area. I was about a block from my building when I noticed a group of young toughs loitering on a corner across the street. One of them yelled out: "Hey! There goes one!"

I had no idea what he meant, but I broke into a dead run, clutching at my hat. My apartment building was owned by an old retired policeman — they often left the force with a great deal of cash in those days in New York, and he had used his to buy the building. The old man heard the racket outside the window and rushed out, brandishing a huge old pistol, and the young hoodlums fled at the sight of it.

I was disenchanted with uptown New York after that so I began to look for another place to live. I had heard wild and wonderful stories about *la vie de bohème* in Greenwich Village, so I finally bought a charming old brownstone house on Charlton Street. Each of the floors was a separate apartment; I lived on the top floor and sublet the others to a widely varied series of people who kept my life from being dull, ever again, in New York.

One of my first tenants was a man I came to regard with misgivings. He had a name in the neighborhood for being a "man about town." I was never really sure what that meant, but I convinced myself it was something underhanded and probably dangerous. He regularly entertained a number of vapid young ladies, rarely the same one twice, and after a while I managed to get rid of him.

The house's respectability was restored when the second floor was rented by a group of earnest women who embroidered church vestments. They were quiet to the point of distraction — I could strain to hear a sound to no avail — but they paid their rent promptly and stayed quite a long time.

Some of the aura of respectability was dissipated when Floyd Dell came from Chicago to live in the basement apartment with a woman who was clearly not his wife. Floyd was a sickly-looking, rather frail man with scant yellow hair and a general look of near degeneracy to him that was, fortunately, deceptive. He roamed about the entire apartment house freely and even managed to make friends with the sewing ladies, who were initially horrified when he simply popped in on them without benefit of invitation. Floyd clearly believed he had full visiting privileges to everyone and was in my apartment one day working on an article for *The Masses* — for some reason he often wrote in my apartment — when there was a knock at the door and I went to answer it. It was someone I had never seen before, a beefy, unpleasant-looking man, and he asked for Floyd Dell.

Behind me, Floyd was grimacing and gesturing that he was not at home to callers, he told me later, but neither the stranger nor I could see him. "How coincidental," I told the man brightly. "He's right here now."

I threw the door open widely to reveal Floyd in the act of a grimace and a gesture.

Without a word the stranger handed Floyd an official-looking document and departed at once. It was a subpoena, of course. Floyd told me he had written some rather controversial articles for *The Masses* about the state of government in the United States, and now the government was quite interested in putting him in jail.

I had little time to mourn Floyd's dilemma, for an exciting thing had happened to me. Miss Plummer of the Library School had introduced me to Mr. Frank Doubleday, an autocratic and distinguished gentleman who wore flawlessly tailored tweeds and carried himself in a grand manner that greatly impressed me. Mr. Doubleday needed someone to take over the running of the Doubleday Doran Bookstore. He was, perhaps, dubious about hiring a woman for the position, but it was the year 1916 and men were more interested in preparing for the war that was obviously brewing in Europe. Mr. Doubleday scrutinized both my credentials and myself and finally decided I was presentable enough to appear in his bookstore and educated enough to be able to operate it, and I became one of the very few women at that time to occupy such a lofty position.

I was worried at first, because I knew nothing of the ordering or selling of books. How would I know which books to buy? It was a risk for both Mr. Double-day and myself, but it worked out very well. The sales-men who came around were very helpful because they liked the idea of having someone sell books who actually enjoyed reading them and could talk to people who were interested. At that time many of the clerks in bookstores had no more interest in books than their price and weight.

The Doubleday Doran Bookstore was magnificent. It was located in what had once been the carriage drive-way of Lord and Taylor on Fifth Avenue and 43rd Street and was a great long corridor, connected to the main store by a huge arch. There was a mosaic tile floor, partly covered with thick, rich Turkish rugs. All the lamps had silk shades and there were a number of comfortable chairs scattered about. After I came to know more about the business, I had the chairs taken away. Certain customers would come in and then simply sit around all day reading as though it were their private club.

At one end of the store was the children's book de-partment, and all the rest of it was used to display reg-ular books. Lord and Taylor customers would come in with their charge accounts which could also be used in the bookstore. They accounted for many of our sales.

The bookstore mostly thrived, of course, on the

Doubleday Doran sets of books, such as the *Little Masterpieces* which were bound in cloth and sold for thirty cents a volume. There were other Doubleday Doran sets, bound in cloth and leather, of such authors as Conan Doyle, Mark Twain and Rudyard Kipling. We also had an incredible number of a dreadful book called *Rebecca of Sunnybrook Farm.*

There was an extraordinary woman who used to phone in and ask if we had any blue books. I was confused at first because I had no idea what she was talking about, but after a time I realized that she would buy any book at all as long as it had something to do with the color blue. If a book were entitled *Bluebeard, The Blue and the Gray, The Mystery of the Blue Lagoon* or *The Bobbsey Twins on Blueberry Hill,* she would order it sight unseen. Even if the jacket of the book were blue, she would buy it. She read them all because she would sometimes comment on a book I sent her and discuss a book on the Civil War with just as much seriousness as the adventures of the Bobbsey Twins. One day she called when we had just run out of blue books to ship off to her. Then I remembered that sets of books could be ordered in any color. I asked if she would take kindly to a complete set of Kipling in blue leather. She was delighted by the idea. I never understood her and never worked up the courage to ask about her curious passion for the color blue.

One man came in and stood around looking at books for so long that I wondered if he were thinking of stealing a few. Finally he came up to me with a very sheepish look on his face and told me what he wanted.

"You know, I just built me a house in the country," he said with a Texas drawl. Then he sighed and explained, "They made all the bookcases half-size for some fool reason and I have to fill them up with something. Is there any way you can think of that I could get some half-size books?"

"Well," I said, hesitating. "There's a warehouse of returned books that aren't going to be sold at Doubleday. I suppose I could ask them to cut some in half for you."

Whoever I spoke to at the warehouse was only too happy to get rid of the unwanted books. They sawed up a batch and shipped them out and I never saw the man in the bookstore again. I have always thought he might have been too embarrassed to return for a book he really wanted to read.

There were many customers who wandered in from Lord and Taylor who simply wanted something to do or something to spend their money on, but gradually we also began to attract customers who were truly interested in books. When they became aware that I shared the same interest they would sometimes come in just to chat.

Around Christmas we became so busy that we had to dig our way through the customers and we were forced to hire extra help. Fortunately, my sister Margaret was going to Wellesley at the time and all her friends wanted to come to New York and work in a bookstore. That was the most thrilling thing they could think of to do, and their mothers thought it would be all right because "Margaret's sister" was running the store. I hired them at Christmas and after they graduated.

It is quite possible that the mothers of these girls visualized me as a sort of housemother who would look after their daughters, but it was a role I sedulously skirted. They came and went too rapidly and I had no time nor inclination to tend to the morals of the girls. They were aggressively mobile and either got married or found much better jobs.

After some time of observing this fact, I realized I was not being paid enough, so I wrote to Mr. Doubleday and said that I should really be earning more money, because all the girls that had left me had gone on to better jobs than I had.

My salary was raised from twenty-five to thirty-five

dollars a week. It was possible to live on that kind of money in those days if you were very careful. My father was generous and I was more than comfortable.

With the additional money came additional responsibilities. I was now expected to attend sales meetings at Doubleday Doran and to come up with ideas about how to sell books and what kind of books to publish. I was not too popular at these meetings because I would usually tell them what I thought of their books.

"How is *Rebecca of Sunnybrook Farm* selling?" they would ask me.

"As well as you might expect," I would respond in a disgusted voice. "I'm not interested in that nonsense. Why don't you publish books I can enjoy selling?"

They thought I was disparaging their list and they were quite right. They resented the idea that a woman might do this, for they were, mostly, dead set in their ways.

Usually I went to the meetings thinking, "Heavens, I don't have a thing to tell them." But at one of the conferences, I suddenly remembered a friend who had just returned from England. She had told me that everybody over there was reading paperbound books.

Without really thinking it through, I said to Mr. Doubleday, "Why don't you publish the same books, but in paper covers and at a lower price?"

31

"Oh nonsense!" he said. "We are not going to lower our standards."

But despite my marked lack of success at the sales meetings, the bookstore was doing very well. Salesmen would drop in to tell me what they had that was new and I would somehow sell the books that I bought. I could be sharp-tongued about books I didn't like, and when I criticized any of the books published by Alfred Knopf it was reported to the higher echelons, for Alfred Knopf would come into the store to try to convince me of the merits of his books, invariably bringing along his beautiful Borzoi dog. He was about my own age and it was always more a social call than a business one. We had many long, interesting talks together, sometimes about books but just as often about dogs, while the Borzoi padded gracefully about the store, as though investigating the line we carried.

Whenever I wanted to know about any of the more technical books, on philosophy or science or some such subject, I would ask my brother David for advice. He was teaching at Amherst College then, and he introduced me to Stark Young, whom he had met there. Stark advised me about art books and we came to be quite friendly. At that time, Stark was a critic for the *New Republic*. The basement in my house was empty when I met him, so he rented it for a time.

Stark had a round, pale face with a rather pointed chin — not at all handsome, but he dressed with great elegance and carried himself grandly. He was an enthusiastic socialite and loved to go to fine places with stunning debutantes, none of whom he took seriously. He was entertaining and gallant, but he also knew a great deal. There was a solid background of intelligence behind the facade of frivolity.

He was rather annoyed at me because I did not care about the social "whirl" and often he sent great ladies into the bookstore in an effort to have me meet them and become friendly with them. They were nice enough, but they seemed to be looking for someone to patronize and I never liked to be patronized.

One very rich girl I had come to know at the bookstore asked me, "Why don't you come to parties once in a while and meet people who are like you?"

"Well, for one thing, they aren't like me," I told her.

"They are," she insisted, then added rather imperiously, "You are coming to see me on Sunday."

I would not be told what I was going to do on Sunday or any other day, so I refused. Later, when I told Stark about the incident, he was furious.

"You shut yourself up in that bookstore too much. Why don't you go out and see people?"

"Let them come and see me," I replied airily.

I did not actually feel all that haughty about it, but I knew it would be impossible to work at the bookstore and then set off on a mad round of parties and drinking and dancing. Besides, I thought I knew many more interesting people. Writers were constantly coming in to check on the sale of their books, and because of the location of the store, many other famous people dropped by. I was surprised to look up one day and find Ethel Barrymore browsing around the book stacks, and even more surprised to learn how well-read and intelligent she was.

One of my friends was Will Cuppy, a plump, elfin young man who lived in a dreadful hole just around the corner from my house. He knew a great many actors who were nearly as poor as he was, and would often bring them all over to have lunch with me on Sundays, when I had time to cook. I enjoyed having them even though I knew they came as much for food as friendliness.

Cup had a strange job of writing reviews of mystery novels for the *New York Times* and was one of the first to realize that a mystery could be an art form. He had an offbeat wit that viewed the world from a tilted slant and many people did not realize he was being very funny until some time after the fact. He affected a pose that he did not know much of anything and that he merely wrote what he thought. Once, after I had met Sherwood Anderson, Cup confided in me, "You know, I can't read Anderson. All he ever writes about is Jim and Joe sitting on a log in the Middle West and talking."

Cup introduced me to the sister of Sherwood Anderson's first wife, and in time, Margaret Lane came to be my dearest friend. Peg was a skilled anesthetist and a very handsome girl as well. She was an unusual friend for me — something of an adventuress, who would dare anything and do anything. We had great fun together though we were totally unlike in temperament and appearance. She was a tall, black-haired beauty who wore striking, vivacious clothes, while I was small and inclined toward quieter colors and more sedate styles.

Peg had an idea that I lived like a nun and I used to try to dissuade her of this by making up long and frankly fantastic stories about adventures that had happened to me. One day, I bought a bunch of violets on my way home and I improvised an improbable tale for her.

"Oh!" I exclaimed, rushing into her room. "What a wonderful thing just happened to me. I was standing on a corner waiting for a bus and there was a young man and his girlfriend standing there too. He was trying to give her these violets but she was angry at him and wouldn't take them. Finally he turned around and handed them to me and then he tried to date me to make the other girl jealous."

Peg did not quite believe me, but I had the bouquet of violets to back up my story. She did not argue about it; she simply proceeded to reel off a story of her own day that was far more inventive and exciting than mine.

None of my Village friends could ever really believe that I enjoyed the time I spent in the bookstore, but it was a good time to be in that kind of business. People genuinely enjoyed reading and many who had never before read for pleasure were now coming to ask me to recommend a good book to them.

Across the street from us, next to the Farmer's Bank where I had an account, there was an old-fashioned club and the old men would sit in the window and get more and more bored. When they were finally submerged to a certain depth in ennui, they got up and creaked over to the bookstore to buy books and talk to me. I had plenty of time for them; it was not a strenuous job except that it was tiring to see quite so many people each day. The old men from the club were a mainstay for the store. They bought armloads of books in return for the pleasure of chatting with the pretty young girls who worked in the store. It was great fun to watch the old men perk up.

Even the book thieves provided excitement. There were almost none of them in the summer, but in the winter they came in droves. They wore bulky coats with great pockets inside and would stand too long at the expensive book counters. When we suspected someone, we had to call a detective down from Lord and Taylor and he would wait by the door until the thief went outside before he arrested him. All the bookstores were suffering from thefts. At first I tried to convince myself that the booknappers were students who needed the books or people who loved them but could not afford to pay for them, but it was not true. The books would be resold the same day they were stolen.

At one point, Mr. Doubleday decided it might be a good thing to add a rare book department and he sent me off to London to look into the possibilities and potentials of the business. I had a fine time on the boat over, but the trip mostly served to show me my own lack of expertise in the rare book field. I just did not know enough about various editions and what was and was not valuable.

My mother still had a few relatives living in Cornwall, which was a nice, warm, comfortable part of England. I went to visit them and found that they did nothing but play croquet all day and talk about it half the night. My father had wielded a crack croquet mallet, so I knew the game and was able to enter into their society. At home we had always played an aggressive, no-holds-barred kind of croquet, but I was astonished at the brand played by my genteel relatives. They maintained an icy aplomb while sending an opponent's ball crashing into an unplayable lie and were ruthlessly intent on winning at any cost.

They were all old people at that time and they introduced me to all their friends as "Janey's child." They rarely called me anything else, as it seemed to be a local custom. One man called his wife "she," never using her name at all. Somehow they thought that "Janey's child" should speak proper English and were dismayed to find that I talked like an American.

When I had my fill of "Janey's child" and croquet, I went back to my bookstore in New York. It was nearly Thanksgiving and we would soon be swamped with Christmas customers.

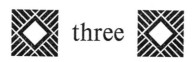 three

Stark Young asked, "Do you need any help in the bookstore? I have a young friend named William Faulkner who wants to stay in New York for a while."

"Of course," I said. "This time of year we always need extra people."

Stark had grown up near Oxford, Mississippi, and had taught at Old Miss. He told me that he had once arranged for Bill Faulkner to take certain special classes there. They were old friends and when Bill came to New York he stayed with Stark for a time. He had been there for several months, picking up odd jobs here and there. One of them, Stark said, had been washing dishes in a Greek restaurant.

I had reservations about that being the right kind of experience for selling books, but the moment I met Bill Faulkner, I knew he would be good at it. He was dressed quite formally — probably in his only suit — and he looked very elegant and distinguished. He fitted perfectly into the genteel atmosphere of the Doubleday Doran Bookstore.

The ladies loved him and would buy anything that he told them was good. He was frightfully aristocratic and had the kind of gallant Southern manners that intimidated customers. At times he could be rude to them and they would love it. "Oh," he would say, "don't read that trash. Here's the book you should have." They would agree to anything — encyclopedias, gardening manuals, Plato — anything at all. They went off with great stacks of books, absolutely thrilled with the young, English-looking man, with his chin tucked down into his tie, very solemn and charming.

Bill and I came to be good friends and I learned that he drank himself to sleep every night. He drank prodigiously but never showed a sign of it. He had found himself a little room in the Village for two dollars and fifty cents a week, and when he could afford it, he would drink most of the night and come up as fresh as a rose in the morning.

He did not have liquor at the bookstore, of course,

but he admitted to me that he started off each day with a glass of White Mule. I gathered that he had grown up on a plantation where the corn liquor was made in great quantities by one of the colored help who did nothing but tend to the fixin's. Bill had more or less grown up with it and had no problems with it at that time.

When Bill waited on one of my regular customers, he would defer to me by saying, "I'll ask Miss Elizabeth." It was certainly not a New York way of addressing people and the customers were either greatly impressed or they thought he was crazy — or that I was. The name caught, however, and eventually followed me to New Orleans, where even my husband would catch himself calling me "Miss Elizabeth."

Bill and I had long talks during lulls in the work, and he would tell me amazing, lurid tales about his life. At first I was shocked by what he was revealing to me, but later I became skeptical. "Bill," I would say, "is that really true?"

He would answer with hurt innocence, "Why, of course it is. Would I lie to you, Miss Elizabeth?"

The answer to that was that of course he would lie to me, whenever it struck his fancy.

Once he told me about his closest friend in Oxford who had married a girl whom Bill was in love with. He claimed that the girl was going to have his baby even though she had married his best friend. I was convinced that there was not a grain of truth in the story but it seemed a good, tragic beginning for fiction. Bill's stories were always very elaborate and detailed and utterly fascinating. I listened to them all and never again let on that I doubted their credibility at all.

Bill disappeared for two or three days at one point, and when he finally showed up I asked him, "Where on earth have you been?"

He said he had been at the seashore, at a resort where people swam and sat around in the sun all day. There was an incredibly beautiful girl who was also staying there and Bill had fallen for her in a big way. The trouble was, he told me, that the girl did not like him at all. He trailed after her and hovered over her but the girl would not come across. As he related the tale, he did a first-rate job of acting brokenhearted over the frustrating affair. He almost wept but I knew he did not mean any of it. He was simply working out, in a novelist's way, how a man feels when some girl turns him down. It was all literary plunder for him, and immensely interesting for me.

In many of his stories I later recognized the beginning of his novels. Certainly, the wild, crazy things I heard fitted perfectly into the baroque texture of his prose.

He had already published the requisite "slim volume" of poetry, called *The Marble Faun*. I thought it was dreadful — kind of a garbled Shelley — but of course I could hardly tell him.

Bill finally left the bookstore because he had been offered a job in Oxford as postmaster, of all things. It turned out that he was a much better bookseller than postmaster, because he just could not be bothered with the day-to-day routine of a post office. He had a huge sack into which he threw all the second-class mail and he did not have it delivered until the sack was full. He had his mind on matters that were loftier than mere letters.

I missed Bill after he left, but my life in the Village was lively enough to fill the void. I met a strange, fey young woman who had come from the Middle West. She told me, as she told everybody, that when she was born her father also had an illegitimate child by his mistress. The ensuing scandal had broken up the family, but her father had perversely insisted on naming both her and her half sister April.

April had come to New York and promptly changed her name to Avril to distinguish herself from the other girl. She opened a tiny place with candles stuck in bottles and served only coffee or hot chocolate and doughnuts. Everybody in the Village went there; it was the thing to do. She was only open in the evenings, to accommodate her natural laziness. She could have taken in only about fifty cents per customer, but a great many people dropped in and she made enough to live on at a minimal level which seemed to suit her nicely.

Avril had the oddest system of housekeeping I have ever seen. She lived in an enormous room furnished only with an enormous bed. Her baby, whose father was conspicuously absent and unmentioned, slept in one half of the bed and Avril slept in the other. She never changed the sheets. Never. She turned her half of the bed down for the night, slept in it, and turned it back in the morning.

Everyone knew this wild-haired, staring-eyed waif of the Village, and through her came to know me. I was distinctly Middle Western and somewhat suspect in the Village. I had a steady job which I enjoyed and I had enough money to live cleanly if not splendidly. I was not at all bohemian enough for their tastes but I gradually became aware that they always came to me when they were broke and needed to borrow money. They did not disdain the working girl when they had a use for her.

This was a time when Maxwell Bodenheim seemed to be lurking about wherever you went. He was a great friend of Avril's and certainly one of the filthiest poets around, physically and poetically. He always looked on the verge of a fatal illness, or just recovering from a near one. He was thin and hunched over as if to shield himself from an impending blow and his darting, suspicious eyes gave the same cringing, fearful impression. Reciting his own poetry was his usual occupation and he always managed to do it at the wrong time and place. If a professor or well-dressed uptowner walked into Avril's hole in the wall by mistake or through curiosity, Maxwell would be there to loudly and hollowly intone the morose phrases he passed as poetry.

There was another man who lived nearby and someone had made the sad error of telling him he looked like Christ. He grew a great shaggy beard on the strength of that, but drew the line at behaving in a Christlike way. I was not a part of that set; I knew them only from a comfortable, perhaps disdainful, distance.

Edna St. Vincent Millay lived a few doors from me, and everyone was delighted with her. She was a lovely, charming creature and hopelessly irresponsible, though no one minded in the least. She always had a coterie of followers but did not care about them one way or the other. She was a brilliant girl, fascinating to listen to as she talked about herself and what she was going to do next.

My house seemed to be filled with friends at all times and we had a clique of our own that had nothing to do with the more garish and outlandish personalities of the Village. Susan Glaspell lived in the house for a while, writing a long book about Greece. A few blocks away lived Max Eastman and his sister Crystal.

Stark Young was often around when he was not otherwise occupied with his society friends. He was always great fun because he knew so much about so many subjects. He could preside over a dinner party and entertain every person there in high style. He had tried so many different things. He had been a teacher of English literature, a critic, a painter and had once tried to write a play for his friends, the Lunts.

Yet to me it seemed that Stark was a deeply disappointed man. He had been fired from Amherst College because of Robert Frost, according to my brother David, who also taught there. Frost had claimed that Stark was an "out and out" homosexual and was therefore unfit to teach in a college with young boys around. It was an idiotic idea, said David, for Stark would not have seduced a male student any more than Frost would have seduced a female one. David believed that Stark talked with the boys with a sympathy that Frost could not manage, and that he helped them a good deal. It was David's idea that Frost was jealous of Stark's popularity, but then David had taken a great dislike to Frost.

Some time later, Stark wrote a number of novels and the one which at first seemed to have the best chance for success was *So Red the Rose*. It was a Civil War novel but unfortunately it was published the same year as *Gone with the Wind*. Stark's book was completely eclipsed, even though it was a fine book, better, I think, than Mrs. Mitchell's.

But in the days when he lived in the basement apartment of my house, Stark managed to conceal any frustration he may have felt. Both he and I listened to Peg Lane as she told us about her ex-brother-in-law Sherwood Anderson, who was a literary figure of some fame, even in those days. Sherwood's new wife was named Tennessee and she was a determinedly "emancipated" woman. They kept separate apartments and were both very liberal and modern. Floyd Dell had also told me about the days in Chicago when he had known Sherwood, and it was natural for me to become interested in hearing more about this great, free spirit of the Midwest, my own territory.

Sherwood came to New York in 1922 because he had been hired to work on a movie that John Emerson was producing. John had grown up with Sherwood in Clyde, Ohio, and his wife, Anita Loos, was also a close friend of "Swatty" as she called him.

Peg Lane and I and Edith Dudley were living together in my apartment on the top floor, and Sherwood visited us often in order to see Peg. Very gallantly he took us all out to dinner. He liked all kinds of women and was always highly susceptible to them. I was somewhat afraid of him. He was a large man, big-boned and rugged, and had a great shock of gray hair. He wore flamboyant clothes and told extravagant, unlikely stories in which he dramatically acted out all the roles.

I paid little attention to him at first because I was so busy, and that may have been the reason he took note of me.

Sherwood kept on coming to the apartment and slowly it dawned on me that he was coming not to see Peg, but me. We got to know each other warily, partly because of my own reticence and partly because Sherwood was on the verge of divorcing Tennessee at that time. He was not prepared to become involved with another woman so soon.

We went out together a few times, always to some odd outré place he had discovered in his rovings. I did not drink, then, but Sherwood would drink enough to feel relaxed and he would talk to me at great length about himself and what he was going to do. He had a sweeping self-confidence that impressed itself deeply on me. I began to feel that this man had a true sense of him-self and what he could accomplish. I recall sitting in dimly lit bistros, as intent on his dark, dark eyes as I was on what he was telling me.

One day Sherwood came to see me in a towering rage. He had just gone, for the first time, to pay a call on Theodore Dreiser at his apartment in St. Luke's Place. Sherwood was an enthusiastic admirer of Dreiser and had written a prose poem to him which he published as the foreword to *Horses and Men*. Sherwood told me that he had gone to Dreiser's apartment several times before but had never been able to get up enough nerve to actually ring the bell.

This time, though, he had finally done it and had waited nervously for Dreiser to answer the door. When he did, Sherwood said, "Hello, I'm Sherwood Anderson. I thought I would come to see you."

Dreiser stared at him for a moment, then said, "Hello," and shut the door in his face. Sherwood stood there for a time, facing the closed door until his shock had changed to anger. Then he rushed out of the building.

I had never before seen Sherwood angry and it frightened me. He cursed Dreiser first, then began to speculate that he had a young girl in his apartment he wanted to keep hidden. Then he wondered if Dreiser could have misinterpreted the prose poem in which he had referred to him as an old man, though not in years.

Finally Sherwood left, and later called to tell me that when he had gone home there was a note from Dreiser explaining that he had simply been embarrassed, just as Sherwood had been to go there at all. The note added that Dreiser had arranged a party for Sherwood to meet some of the interesting men in the city.

Sherwood went to the party eagerly, and there were a number of writers he had been wanting to meet, including Henry Mencken, Carl Van Vechten, Ernest Boyd and Llewelyn Powys. They all sat around on chairs that were lined up along the walls as if the room were a dance hall. They were chatting in small groups for nearly two hours before Mencken asked Dreiser about the liquor that had been set out. Dreiser had not invited anyone to have a drink. Dreiser just laughed and said they should have enough sense to help themselves.

Later that night, F. Scott Fitzgerald, who had somehow heard about the party and who wanted to pay his respects to Dreiser, rang the doorbell. Dreiser went to answer it, opened the door and stood staring at the young author whose name was so much in the literary limelight at that time.

Fitzgerald introduced himself and held out some bottles of champagne he had brought with him as a sort of offering. Dreiser took the champagne, said "Hello," and closed the door in Fitzgerald's face, just as he had done earlier to Sherwood. He had been unable to find a way to graciously invite the writer in, though he was aware that everyone at the party would have been pleased to meet him.

Another time Sherwood was walking around in New York when a sudden inspiration hit him. It was in the early morning and he happened to be close to Stark Young's apartment. Sherwood went directly to it and rang the bell. Stark was just about to go out and Sherwood asked if he could sit in the apartment for a time. All he wanted was paper and pen and solitude. Stark was not at all put out by the request. He promptly produced paper and pen and a bottle of whiskey, then provided solitude by quietly leaving.

In the late afternoon, Stark returned to his apartment. Sherwood had indeed been writing. There were sheets of paper tossed all over the place, under the bed in the bedroom, in the kitchen, on the floor. The table where Sherwood had been writing was littered with papers and the bottle of whiskey was completely empty. Stark looked around and found Sherwood lying, pale and sleeping, fully dressed in his bed.

At first Stark was sure that Sherwood was ill and he

shook him lightly to waken him. "What happened?" Stark asked when Sherwood sat up.

Sherwood shook his head groggily and told Stark that he had been trying for years to write a certain story. Suddenly that morning, for no reason he could explain, the story came through to him and he had been obsessed with the need to write it down immediately. He had been drinking from the bottle as he wrote, not knowing if it were whiskey or cold coffee. It had no effect on him at all until he had finished the story.

I had come to realize that Sherwood was a man who was unlike anyone I had known before. He was both impressive and impressionable, exciting and excitable. It was impossible to tag him with a label, — he was never the same person from day to day. He had to be accepted for the mood he happened to be in at the moment, and slowly I was beginning to accept him. It was a grudging process, for I did not want the order of my life to be shattered.

Sherwood loved to walk and we took long strolls around New York, sometimes silent, sometimes talking. I never had any idea what to expect from him next. He might say, "Come on, let's have dinner at a place out on Staten Island. I can't remember the name of it, but it's a great place and I can find it easily."

And we would take a subway to the Staten Island Ferry and cross over, standing out on the deck while Sherwood gulped down the fresh air as though he wanted all that he could drink in.

On Staten Island we would walk, seemingly for hours, until we came to a woods or a pasture that suited Sherwood's fancy. There were fine, wild places to stroll through then, and Sherwood loved the idea of being in the country.

But it usually turned out that he was completely unable to find the hotel or restaurant he was looking for and we would sit around in some park, talking endlessly and starving to death. When I became desperate, we would finally eat in the first lunch counter we came to, good or bad.

After some time of this I made up my mind that I did not want to fall in love with this man; I had a comfortable, pleasant life in New York with comfortable, pleasant friends. Even in the short time I had known Sherwood, I could feel the focal point of my interest shifting. The bookstore no longer seemed so very important to me. I told Sherwood firmly that I would not go out with him again. After that, I did not see him for a few days, but then he came back and it started all over again.

This was repeated several times and then I realized it was too late. I was in love with Sherwood and there was nothing to do about it.

Peg Lane was just about to go off on a vacation for a few weeks and she dropped into the bookstore on the day she left. She had always been so positive that I would marry Stark Young. When she came into the bookstore, it was crowded with customers and all I had time to do was to wave at her. She came halfway into the store, then stopped and called out over the heads of my customers: "All I want to know is — which one is it going to be? S.A. or S.Y.?"

Without hesitating a moment, I called back: "S.A."

Peg was not at all upset about the news but S.Y. was. He said to me, "Miss Elizabeth, I just don't think you belong in that kind of life."

I suppose Stark was right. It did not do me any great harm as so many of my friends thought it would, but it was difficult at times.

Sherwood's wife Tennessee may have started out wanting complete freedom for both partners in her marriage, but she had evidently changed her mind. Her liberalism did not encompass giving up Sherwood easily. She knew many people in New York and she spread the word around that it was my fault that Sherwood was divorcing her.

Sherwood had told me that he had made up his mind to divorce Tennessee long before he had met me and I believed him. But Tennessee was not convinced and she started a rumor that I was running a den of iniquity in the Village, with homosexuals living on one floor and myself on another, living in sin with Sherwood.

None of it was true but I could not let it continue, so I decided to join my parents in California, which was where they had moved. I wanted to give Sherwood time to resolve his marriage completely before I saw him again. I resigned from Doubleday Doran and gave up my house in the Village. I packed together my belongings and boarded a train for a trip that grew lonelier as the days and the country went by.

I had been so sure that I had established the pattern of my life: I was to continue on as the manageress of the Doubleday Doran Bookstore, living out my days amid a circle of brilliant friends and a wider circle of famed acquaintances. But Sherwood had flashed through the circle like a meteor and had drawn me along in his wake. I was thirty-eight years old and irreversibly committed to a man of forty-seven. Like a teen-ager, I was running away from my home in New York to find adventure.

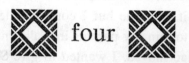 **four**

My family greeted me in Berkeley with a rousing welcome and a sheaf of letters that Sherwood had already sent to me. I read them all with great eagerness, for by then I was feeling the strange emptiness of separation. Into the letters he poured all his miseries, his passions, his poetry, in pages and pages of scrawled, almost illegible handwriting.

He had to have his way. It was a basic part of his nature and a childish part perhaps. If conditions were not precisely for him, he sank into profound depressions and what he wanted right now was to be rid of his former wife and to marry me. Nothing less would do.

To this end, he wrote, he had decided to take up residence in Reno in order to divorce Tennessee. He expected to be there only a few months.

As it turned out he was forced to stay for over a year because Tennessee was bitterly opposing the divorce by demanding that a large sum of money be paid to her at some undefined time in the future.

Sherwood had explained the situation to me. He had not been very happy in his marriage almost from the start and at one point he had run away from Tennessee to a little town named Fairhope, across the bay from Mobile, Alabama. Tennessee had followed him there, abruptly appearing at the little retreat he had found. He was annoyed, but could not send her away. To give her something to do, he provided her with clay and showed her how to work with it. He sat with her, telling her about the characters in a book he was writing and encouraged her to try to sculpt her conception of the people he described. She followed his instructions and made a number of heads which were photographed and later used as illustrations for Sherwood's book *The Triumph of the Egg*.

Now Tennessee wanted to be paid for the illustrations, and paid handsomely. Sherwood had no great amount of money and had no visions of it in the future, so he certainly could not commit himself to an obligation like that. Instead, he stayed on, more or less trapped in Reno.

I received a continuing flood of letters from Sherwood, all of them insisting that I join him in Reno. I thought that it was a terrible thing for such a man to be so unhappy and distraught. He needed peace and a feeling of security and I knew that I wanted to try to provide him with that. I decided to go to Reno. Sherwood urgently wanted someone to be with him and hold his hand.

When I told my family I was going to Reno they were shocked, as I expected them to be, but it was what I wanted to do and I knew that they would eventually accept the idea. But it was very much against my family's advice that I set out for Reno.

Sherwood had only been in Reno for a few weeks when I arrived and he was staying in a small hotel. I rented a hideous little cottage, identical to the many other hideous little cottages that had been thrown up to house potential divorcées. There was a small sitting room, not designed to be used much, a bedroom, kitchen, and dining room. Sherwood retained his room at the hotel but ate all his meals with me and used the dining room for his writing.

My brother David had been afraid that Tennessee

might give us trouble by raising a scandal about my presence in Reno, but she evidently had more sense than that. There was no ground for a scandal, for we had to be reasonably careful. At one point, David came out to visit me, and when Sherwood came that day I rushed out of the house to meet him. Sherwood took me into his arms and we kissed. David was horrified, for the house was on a hill where everybody could see it.

"For heaven's sakes," he said. "You mustn't carry on like that in front of the neighbors. Wait till you're married. Or at least until you're inside the house."

In Reno I came to know Sherwood very well. He spent long hours telling me of his life before he met me, and although I later heard him alter the facts for dramatic effect or sheer perversity, I believe he told me as much of the truth as was still recognized by him.

He had been born on September 13, 1876, in Camden, Ohio. His mother, Emma Smith, was a sturdy, sensible German girl and his father, Irwin, was a jovial, irresponsible man who drifted from harness making to house and sign painting. Sherwood led an odd life of poverty and hardship in his youth, for his father was never able, or perhaps willing, to provide the family with sufficient money to live comfortably. When they moved to Clyde, Ohio, in 1884, Sherwood's mother took in washing when she had to, and Sherwood had been bitterly resentful when he was forced to carry dirty laundry from and clean laundry to neighboring houses.

Emma Anderson was not a warm or affectionate woman but she dominated the lives of her children, Karl, Stella, Sherwood, Irving, Ray and Earl. She had a steel-hard core of determination and managed, with only casual help from her husband, to raise her six children in a manner she thought proper. Much later, I was to hear Sherwood describe his mother as a "passionate Italian" and his father as a "ruined Southerner" and he exaggerated the extreme poverty of his family. But in Reno, intent on revealing himself to me, Sherwood told me of a family that teetered on the brink of desperation but never plunged over the side.

Sherwood described his mother as a silent sufferer, a woman whose health was being ruined by overwork and childbearing, but a woman of great endurance and resolve. Irwin, Sherwood's father, was regarded by the citizens of Clyde as a likable man, but too inclined to "toots" to take seriously — he was a charmer, not a worker. Sherwood was a critical and serious-minded boy and his father's reputation as a clownish ne'er-do-well humiliated him. This may have been why Sherwood's own public "image" came to be so vitally important to him.

As a boy, Sherwood developed an aggressive indus-

made many spelling and grammatical errors, which was only to be expected considering his erratic education, and Cornelia pointed them out to him, thereby earning his enmity. He began to think that she was hostile to the idea of his writing, which may have been the case, since it was, in fact, threatening his success as a businessman. He had the idea that he could run the business on charm alone and that he could persuade people to do whatever he wanted them to do, while he devoted his true energies to his art. Eventually the business began to fail, and debts began to mount. Sherwood was faced with a seemingly insoluble dilemma. If he did not give up his writing, his business would fail, but he could not simply call a halt to the creative drive that grew in him. He manufactured what must have seemed to him to be the perfect solution: He feigned madness and vanished.

No one ever knew the complete truth behind Sherwood's famous seizure of amnesia. Sherwood told so many versions of it that I do not believe he knew the truth himself, after a time. He simply walked out of his office after telling his secretary, "My feet are cold and wet. I have been walking too long on the bed of a river." For four days he wandered aimlessly about the countryside until he was found in a shabby hotel in Cleveland, four days later.

At first he described it as amnesia, but later he invented a more sophisticated malady he called "conscious aphasia." In Reno, he admitted to me that he realized his business was failing because he no longer wanted to have anything to do with it. He thought his creditors might be easier on him if they thought he was really sick.

Sherwood moved his wife and family to Chicago, where he earned a living as a copywriter for an advertising agency, but spent his time and energy writing. His marriage to Cornelia lasted a few more years, but she wanted him to be the businessman she had married and he had changed irrevocably. Sherwood no longer cared about breadwinning. Cornelia found work as a schoolteacher in Indiana to earn money to raise their three children. They were divorced in 1916 and Sherwood married Tennessee Mitchell, a music teacher and a burning idealist. She had been named for an early suffragist, Tennessee Claflin, and she shared the beliefs of her namesake. Sherwood and Tennessee promised each other that their marriage was to be without restrictions; each was to come and go at will, with none of the onerous responsibilities that Sherwood had come to hate so much.

Sherwood began publishing short stories and articles in several literary magazines, and in 1916 his first novel, *Windy McPherson's Son,* was published. After that he published *Marching Men* in 1917, *Mid-American Chants* in 1918, *Winesburg, Ohio* in 1919, *Poor White* in 1920, *The Triumph of the Egg* in 1921, and *Many Marriages* in 1923, which was when he was in Reno. By that time he had established a solid literary reputation.

I was worried and disturbed by Sherwood's account of his past life and I spent many hours wondering about my own future with him. Both of his previous wives had tried to dominate Sherwood — Cornelia with her fears that his career as a writer might interfere with his career in business, and Tennessee with her insistence that Sherwood *be* somebody. Once she tried to make him read *Death in Venice* and to use Thomas Mann as a guide for his prose style.

Finally I decided that I knew what Sherwood wanted and needed. He needed to be managed, not dominated. He wanted someone to make his world right for him, to cook his meals, clean his house, to love him without demanding. I had been independent all my life and I thought I could provide him with all of this. His other wives had tried to change him. I would try to adapt myself to him.

Certainly in Reno we were wonderfully happy. Reno

65

itself had little to recommend it but its lax divorce laws. It was an ugly little town with none of the later tinseled glamor of the casinos and gambling palaces.

What made up for the drabness of the town was the country that surrounded it. We were in a large valley, shaped like a pan, at an altitude of around five thousand feet. The air was thin and clear and as exhilarating as the icy water from a mountain stream. As in all high places, the light changed the landscape constantly and quickly so that we could look up at the mountains and see all their aspects changing before our eyes.

Sherwood acquired a secondhand Dodge roadster and was practicing driving it around in the fields until he thought he could manage it well enough to take it on the road. He drove onto the highway and it went along well enough for a time, then suddenly it stopped and he could not make it go. He had no idea what was wrong with it, so he walked to the nearest garage and had the car hauled in.

The mechanic looked it over and said, "Well, you ain't got no gas. That's why it stopped."

Sherwood said, "Oh. Well, fill it up."

"But you ain't got no oil in there either," the mechanic said.

"Put oil in too."

66

"No water neither."

"Water too," Sherwood echoed.

Finally the car was ready to go and Sherwood got behind the wheel. The mechanic put his foot on the running board and leaned over to look into Sherwood's face. "A while back you told me you write books."

"That's right."

The mechanic shook his head. "God knows what you put in them books, mister, cuz you sure don't know nothing."

Sherwood was greatly pleased by this and told the story for a long time afterward. We drove around in the Dodge nearly every day, sometimes going on up into the mountains and finding grassy meadows ringed with pines. On one such venture we ran into a heavy snowstorm and the snow was piled up on the windshield and hood. As we drove back down, the snow gradually changed to sleet, then rain, and finally a warm rain was pattering down on the roof of the car. It was like being able to choose the season we wanted and then driving into it.

In the fall the nights were comfortably cold for sleeping and the days were sunny and warm. There were subtly shaded sage deserts that stretched for miles to the distant mountains. The gullies that penetrated deep into the mountains had colors that ranged from dead white to fiery reds and dark greens.

Sherwood was totally wrapped up in the scenery and it inspired him to take up painting, which he did with great spirit but, I fear, little talent.

Stark Young sent me a painting and Sherwood decided he could improve on it. Without asking me, he painted over various parts of it. I was furious about this, but then, the original painting was rather like Stark himself, overly romantic and deeply Southern, with crumbled columns and roses in the moonlight. It was nothing I really cherished but what Sherwood turned it into was nothing I could even tolerate.

In the winter the weather turned cold, and with plenty of time on my hands, I decided to take up sewing again. I was good at it and I enjoyed it as well. I had an idea that Sherwood would look well in blue shirts; they would bring out the intense Italian brown of his eyes. I made him a number of blue linen shirts and Sherwood was delighted with them.

He liked the shirts so much that he came to be interested in the process of making them. At first he would help me in small ways, threading needles or snipping loose threads. Finally he began trying to make a shirt himself and actually succeeded in doing it. I suppose he would have been aghast if anyone had dropped in and caught the two of us, sitting in the tiny dining room, both sewing away at blue shirts. But he was proud that he had been able to do it. He liked being able to do all sorts of things.

We made a few friends in Reno and went on picnics in the spring when the weather was warmer. Near the town was an extraordinarily beautiful lake and we would go to it to look and to marvel. It was set in a deep basin and was a pure, shimmering blue completely surrounded by bright yellow sand. Sometimes we would go at night, in the moonlight, to discover an entirely changed, entirely lovely lake.

We found many things to do and one of them was going to the racetracks. Sherwood lived so very much in his mind and imagination that he really thought he knew all about horses, though he had never ridden a horse. But he would throw himself into such interests and soon find out enough to pass as an expert.

Carson City was not far away and we drove there through the green sage desert. The Indians came down in the fall of the year to pick piñon nuts and carry them off in great sacks. It seemed they lived on them in bad times and still do. The Indians around Reno were terribly poor and badly taken care of, and I remember feeling a great pity for them. They had been pushed out of their own country and had been reduced to these ragged creatures scavenging for piñon nuts.

Our life in Reno was not entirely an idyl. Sherwood was capable of cruelty, not consciously, but because he was so much wrapped up in his own thoughts and emotions he could not realize the effects of some of his actions on others.

We were walking along the street in Reno one day and an automobile drove past us and parked a short distance away. Sherwood spotted the driver, who was a very pretty young woman, and without a word to me, he went over to the car, leaving me standing alone on the sidewalk. He did not bother to introduce me to the girl, but stood there talking to her for fifteen or twenty minutes.

I was furious. I walked downtown and wandered around until it was time for lunch. I ate in a diner and it was the first meal that I had not prepared for Sherwood. When I finally went home, he had no idea why I was angry. He honestly did not realize he had been rude.

"You beast," I said, with amusement eating at the edges of my anger. "How do you think people can live with you if you behave like that?"

Immediately Sherwood became very contrite and

said he had forgotten to introduce me because the girl was nobody at all. He had never even noticed that she was pretty, if she was. He became extravagant in his apologies, turning the whole thing into a joke. Finally I laughed and cooked lunch for him. I knew he would not eat unless someone made the meal for him. He would not even think about it or notice that it was lunchtime.

Sherwood was quite oblivious to many of the more ordinary aspects of everyday life. At first I had expected him to react to how I looked or what I wore but I soon learned that he could not be bothered. He would be vaguely aware of the color of the dress I had on but that was about all. If I looked disappointed enough, long enough, when I had a new dress he might admit that it was a nice dress. No more. These were minor complaints I knew and quite often I would feel petty for even being aware of them. There was so much that we had together that was fine. Sherwood was a man of intense moods. When he was happy he was irrepressible, bubbling over like a boy, and when he was depressed, gloom hung over him like a pall. For the most part, then, he was happy and far less aggressive and self-assertive than he had been in New York.

In April of 1924, Sherwood's divorce was granted and we prepared to leave. Neither of us was sorry to go.

It was a beautiful country and we had been happy there, but we had been planning our future for so long that we wanted to get on with it. We had discussed the idea of moving to Europe, but Sherwood's literary and emotional roots were planted deep in America and that was all he cared to write about. We gave up the idea of South America for the same reason.

After much thought, we settled on New Orleans. Sherwood had been there two years before and had loved it. He said he wanted to live near the wharves so he could fully enjoy the "ships and darkies." Sherwood had a deep and affectionate feeling for Negroes but not, I think, the kind that would be acceptable in these times.

We wanted to avoid all the publicity we could, so my brother David arranged for us to be married in a small town outside Berkeley, California, where he was now teaching.

It was a brief, almost curt, ceremony and I was rather impressed that Sherwood had been organized enough to get the license, but I suppose David had a hand in that. There had never been any talk about a wedding ring, and I had to buy it myself. Sherwood did not enjoy dealing with details. I gave him a watch and he gave me some piece of jewelry. I did not much care for it and never wore it, knowing he would not notice, but I kept it for a long time.

We left almost immediately after the ceremony for San Francisco, narrowly missing a number of reporters who had somehow heard about the marriage. In those days, writers were regarded as newsworthy, the way that actors are today. The antics of F. Scott Fitzgerald were often headlined and college students pasted photographs of Edna St. Vincent Millay on their walls.

Sherwood was the major American writer of that time. He had broken though the barriers of convention to write of the dark, secret parts of peoples' souls and his books were highly controversial. His position in modern literature is, perhaps, one of influence rather than achievement, for he had abandoned the flowery, elaborate prose of the then popular novelists and had freed other writers to do the same thing.

It was not very surprising, then, that reporters flocked to my brother's house in Berkeley to ask about Sherwood. David told them, "You're too late. They've already gone."

One of the more cynical reporters said, "Come on now, we know that's not true. Bring them out!"

David was outraged. He was a small man, rather mild in appearance, but now he bristled indignantly and his dark eyes flashed behind his wire-rimmed spectacles. He was a professor of philosophy at the University of California and was not accustomed to having his word doubted. "You think I lie?" he snapped.

His wrath was convincing enough to send the reporters away, but it made little difference — the news was in all the papers anyway. Reporters loved Sherwood's curious capacity for publicity. Because his books were regarded as "dirty" in certain circles, he was a figure of public interest.

When we returned from San Francisco, he joked with the newsmen about having eluded them so cleverly, then settled into a chair and told them what they wanted to hear. He had a quick wit and a flair for making quotable remarks. It was only a short time before they were all talking and drinking like good friends.

We stayed on in Berkeley for a time, with my mother and Margaret, who was teaching music at Mills College. Dorothea lived next door with her husband, Max Radin, who was also a professor at the university.

My family wanted us to build a home nearby and join the "compound," but I was quite sure that would not work out too well. I did not think my mother liked Sherwood very much. My father had died some years before and he might have understood Sherwood better, but to Mother, he was somewhat frightening. She was not at all accustomed to the kind of emotional violence that Sherwood could generate. When he got into a discussion with David, it would soon turn into an argument, with both Sherwood and David expounding their views furiously — almost fanatically. Mother simply could not understand that Sherwood lunged at everything he did. Others might eat an apple; Sherwood *experienced* it. His total absorption in his passion of the moment affected others as well, for if David wanted to disagree with Sherwood, he had to do so violently or he would not even be noticed. Mother took note of this, of course, and it must have seemed to her that Sherwood was a disruptive element in her normally quiet world.

There was a great gap between the members of my family and Sherwood. He had very little formal education and it contrasted strikingly with the bookishness of my family. Sherwood read a great deal and knew more about the Russian novelists than any of my family, but there were other areas about which he knew nothing at all.

None of this mattered, for Sherwood had so many other fine qualities and accomplishments, but he thought it did, particularly when he made some error in his talking.

My sister Margaret taught *solfège* at Mills and Sherwood thought she had said "soft edge." Margaret said,

"That's a good name for it." My family had never been restrained in their humor and they laughed a long time over this.

Sherwood looked blank, then puzzled and finally hurt. He still could not see the joke. Margaret quickly said, "It's only natural, Sherwood. After all you don't read French. *Solfège* refers to the sol-fa syllables on the tones of the scale. And it *does* sound like soft edge."

Sherwood tried to laugh about it but could not quite manage.

Dorothea's husband, Max Radin, was an immensely erudite scholar. We never bothered with encyclopedias. We would simply ask Max about whatever we wanted to know. He wrote books about Talmudic law and was a marvelous addition to our family because he loved to talk and it was an education to listen to him. He had the oddest sense of humor I have ever encountered, which was one of the reasons my mother did not much care for him.

Sherwood did not get along with Max very well either. Max had, for Sherwood, committed the cardinal sin. He considered himself something of a critic and one day told Sherwood what he thought was wrong with his latest book, *Horses and Men*. Sherwood could not endure adverse criticism. He once asked me to look through his reviews, only showing him the ones that were favorable.

He said he made himself miserable enough without having others do it for him.

David and Sherwood got on splendidly. They were both solidly behind the workingman. I tried to tell them they did not know what workingmen were really like, not being laborers themselves. But they felt that the closer you got to the earth, the better you were. I thought it was nonsense and said so. They paid no attention to me at all, blithely carried away with the idea that dirt farmers were the salt of the earth and coal miners the spice.

Finally I said, "The pair of you ought to go outside and root around in the dirt and just see how much good it does your souls."

We had other arguments and some wonderful times, because Sherwood could be great fun. Mother liked that side of him, but she was also afraid that since he had been married twice before, he might tire of me too after a while. I should have suspected that too perhaps, but I did not.

Sherwood had his own sense of morality which had nothing to do with conventional thinking. He was not immoral or amoral — just other-moraled. This was apparent in all that he did — his business dealings, his marriages, his manners, and even the games that he played. Once he was playing a game of double solitaire with David in which the point of the game was to finish first. Sherwood just bulled his way through the game, putting his cards down wherever he pleased.

Finally David decided it was impossible to play cards with Sherwood. Mildly, he said, "Well, of course, if you don't follow the rules. . . ."

Sherwood was taken aback. It had never occurred to him that you could not just go right ahead and do whatever you had to in order to win the game.

There was a feeling of solidarity about my family that intrigued and fascinated Sherwood but he could not really understand it. Max had a little girl named Rea from a former wife and the child was regarded as part of our family. She was in high school then and had in her possession a piece of finely sculptured metal. Someone at school saw her with it and just could not believe that a girl of her age could have something so valuable. The superintendent called her down to his office and accused her of having stolen it.

Rea was terribly upset about the affair and Max was furious. We all rose in a body to defend Rea and Sherwood was astonished. He had never before known anything like this kind of family loyalty.

He had lived a lonely life and his family had been so hardworking and scattered that they had never had any time for this kind of unity. He thought that the idea of a family instinctively rising up to defend one of their own was wonderful, but it was a strange phenomenon to him.

He asked me, "Are other people like this too?"

I said, "All the other people I know are."

Sherwood had centered much of his writing on loneliness, something he had felt deeply as a boy, trying to earn enough to live on and learning little underhanded tricks without even knowing that they were wrong. He had an idea that loneliness was an integral part of the spirit of America, and perhaps he was made uncomfortable to know that it was not entirely true.

Everyone was slightly relieved when we left for New Orleans, I think. My family could not manage to shake off a vague feeling of unease around Sherwood, and he was happy to be wandering again, a necessary condition for his peace of mind.

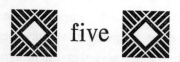 **five**

New Orleans was unlike anything I had seen before and I was immediately enthralled with it. The silver-gray, hanging strands of Spanish moss made even an ugly tree look graceful and lazy and somehow very Southern. The Latin Quarter was bustling and busy, with rattling streetcars and honking automobiles, street vendors calling out their wares with a music that was new to me. The narrow streets were crowded with artists and prostitutes and writers and nuns and easily recognizable tourists with glazed eyes and gaping mouths. Speakeasies flourished openly, and far into the night their music blared out and mingled on the still busy streets. There was a rich, spicy aroma made up of coffee roasting, seafood and the winy-beery smell of the bars.

Sherwood had already rented an apartment in the old Pontalba Building that had been built by the Baroness de Pontalba in 1849. It was a great complex of apartments, with dark, cavernous hallways leading to bright, sunny patios. We stepped out of the sunlight into the immediate coolness of the hall and climbed two flights of narrow, steep stairs. Our apartment had a sweeping view of the city and of Jackson Square directly below. Off to the left was the St. Louis Cathedral with its three spires pointing into the flat green sky of the gathering dusk. A while later, Jackson Square was a lake of green where jellyfish-round lights floated over silver mimosa and hibiscus that blended into oleander and azaleas. Silhouetted against the sky, the palms were like skyrockets, frozen in black explosion.

I could hear a streetcar moving toward us, softly at first, but with an increasing clatter that was a grinding roar of metal on metal as it passed, then faded away again. I caught a glimpse of its name — "Desire." I went about the place, exclaiming over the impossibly high ceilings and fine wrought iron work that was among the best in a city famous for it.

Sherwood wandered off to find out more about the

building and, in particular, the bar on the ground floor. In a short time he came back and said that he had met the owner of the bar, who was a good fellow and a bootlegger besides. "I told him he could store some of his liquor up here," Sherwood said. "He doesn't have room for it in his own place."

"Sherwood, you can't do that," I said quickly.

"What's wrong?" he asked. "Why do you object to it?"

"Well, for one thing, you'd have all kinds of crazy people trooping through here. And you might even get arrested. They'd think it was your own liquor."

He thought about this gravely and then agreed I was probably right. I was to have many such close calls in the future. Sherwood was an impulsive and generous man, inclined toward extravagant gestures. If I could approach such matters delicately I could sometimes manage to temper his rashness. There were many compensations, certainly. Sherwood made friends with everyone, quickly and easily, and we soon knew all of New Orleans.

After a time we moved to a house at 540B St. Peter's Street, which was near the wharves that Sherwood loved so much. A small literary magazine named the *Double-Dealer* was being published in New Orleans by Lillian Marcus Friend, and Sherwood would meet each month with Julius Friend, James Feibleman and Jack McClure to make up the issue. If they did not have enough manuscripts, they would all set about writing enough to fill the edition. Usually, though, they had plenty of material. New Orleans was a literary center of sorts and there were many young writers and artists living nearby.

It was a social and congenial time, with clusters of people meeting to eat at one of the less expensive restaurants, such as Gallatoire's, dining on hot, spicy foods which were complemented by cold wines. Later, everyone would move over to a place called Max in the Alley, a newspaper hangout, with a large ceiling fan that languorously revolved, stirring flies into brief action and casting moving shadows on the walls. It is a scene that is still vivid in my memory, with all the men dressed in rumpled, messy seersucker suits, patched with perspiration and giving the curious effect of a group of people sitting about in white pajamas. There would be William Spratling, looking as slight and dark as a Mexican, with his jutting jaw and eyes that squinted half defiantly at the world; Frans Blom, the anthropologist, with lank brown hair drifting casually over his high forehead and his light-colored eyes staring as if in interested amazement; Oliver La Farge, thin and spindly, all head and thick glasses; Roark Bradford, looking preoccupied and harassed as if all the news of all the world filtered through his active mind into the *Times-Picayune*, which he edited; Hamilton Basso, lithe and handsome with a flashing grin that was startlingly white against his dark tan; Lyle Saxon, who looked aristocratically remote even in a seersucker suit that dared not rumple when worn by him; George Marion O'Donnell and George Milburn, who are somehow blended into the background of my memory. And there would be Sherwood, massive and burly as a bear, with his light cotton jacket twisted and wrinkled impossibly. Sherwood was the only one of them who had an established literary reputation in those days and the younger writers gravitated to him and usually deferred to him, even in the matter of seating, for he was the center of the conversation, always.

We met Bill Spratling through Caroline Durieux, an artist from an old Creole family who had taken Bill under her wing and had shown him around to the various museums, instructing him in what was good and what was bad. Bill taught at Tulane University and lived at Number 264 Pirate's Alley, just down the street from our place, and at the rear of the St. Louis Cathedral.

Bill Faulkner showed up in New Orleans one day with Phil Stone, a lawyer who believed in Bill enough to support him, at least partially. When they arrived, Sherwood was off on a lecture tour, but we had an uproarious week together. They stayed in a funny little hotel with rickety rooms that opened onto a ramshackle courtyard, but they ate all their meals with me. We had an accomplished cook who created a marvelous cuisine.

At night, we would roar around town, seeing crowds of people, exploring murky bistros along Bourbon Street, and sometimes going to a movie theater that catered only to colored people. The theater was located on Rampart Street, which was a marvelous place of shops, cafes, nightclubs and open markets. Here the famous Negro bands originated, which played at funerals and led the parade at carnival time. The movies that were shown in the theater were always Westerns and always dreadful. The worst movies made in Hollywood were projected in this Negro theater, I suppose because they could not be shown anyplace else. It was a horrible, stuffy place, but we sat in the balcony, joking about the good guys and the bad guys and laughing ourselves to a point of near nausea. One night the two Bills, Spratling and Faulkner, and a few other young writers held a foot-race over the rooftops of the Quarter, but I cannot recall who won it, if, indeed, anyone did.

It was a lighthearted interlude of talk and laughter, but the life in the Quarter was one of productivity. In New York I had known so many artists and writers who did nothing but talk of art and writing. In New Orleans, everyone was actively involved in doing something and in trying to do it well.

Sherwood would wake early in the morning and work until around noon; it was a schedule that was followed by many of the people we knew. Late afternoon was the time for being social, and we lived in a house that seemed designed for it. The main part of the house was dank and gloomy, but we lived in what had once been the slave quarters, behind it. It was a charming spot with a small balcony and a patio where everyone would sit around and talk. There was no such thing as a formal party; no one was ever invited, for that would make it seem as though they had to be invited before they would be welcome.

Natalie Scott would drop in to pick up tidbits for her very social column in the *Times-Picayune*, and she would always be gratified, for we were a fine source of news. Her deadline was Saturday noon, but she never turned in any copy until around five in the afternoon. She would invariably discover too many new items she simply had to include. She was a big, sturdy woman who looked as if she had to be efficient, but she was forever losing bits and scraps of paper with vital notes on them, and fluttering furiously through her notebook to find something she had wanted to remind herself about.

Lyle Saxon also worked for the *Picayune*. He was older than most of our New Orleans friends, and probably the person I knew best. He was an enormously tall Southerner with exquisite manners. He was not handsome but very distinguished. He had a beautiful apartment in which he kept a collection of valuable antiques he had inherited from a nearly extinct family.

Lyle gave us a bed that was too huge to fit into his own apartment. It was the largest bed I had ever seen, with mahogany posts and knobs the size of cabbages. There were big brass ornaments and a great velvet canopy that was pleated in the center and draped like a stage curtain. I told Sherwood that the simple act of bedding down now felt like opening night.

I had a feeling at times that Bill Faulkner's studied courtesies and Southern mannerisms were a pose, but that was not true of Lyle. His charming and gallant behavior was a reflection of what he truly felt, which is extremely rare.

Lyle wrote from time to time, but mostly he was an aristocrat and felt no further need to justify his existence. He had lived on plantations most of his life, so that was the background for much of his fiction. One such story was about a Negro who had run off for a day and was walking along a dusty country road with nothing to eat in his pockets but a can of tomatoes, which he drank, then licked the rim of the can. He sent it off to *Dial* and it was returned by Harriet Munroe with a note saying that she liked it but that it would have to be revised because it was too vulgar.

Lyle showed me her rejection slip, and despite the fact that he was crestfallen about it, I had to laugh at the absurdity of the idea of any vulgarity creeping into anything Lyle had written. I assured him that he would never have to worry about any such possibility.

Roark Bradford came around less often because he was kept busy at the *Times-Picayune*. The paper allowed him ten dollars a week to spend on material by local writers, and each week he would hand it over to Bill Faulkner who would turn out short stories and tall tales for him.

Jack McClure also wrote a regular Sunday column for the *Picayune* called "Literature and Less." As one of the editors of the *Double-Dealer*, he encouraged Bill Faulkner to write and published a series of his short sketches called "New Orleans" in January and February of 1925. The *Double-Dealer* also published some of the first works of Ernest Hemingway, and Henry Mencken wrote that the magazine was delivering the South from a cultural swamp.

Hamilton Basso lived at home with his family and had no money at all except what he could borrow here and there. He rarely gave much thought to returning the borrowed money, but he was young and very excited about writing. It is a fine and fetching thing for a young man to be so caught up in what he is doing and Sherwood loved talking to him.

Sherwood enjoyed hugely his position as the center of attention at the gatherings. He would take over the floor to tell a long, rambling story and no one would dare interrupt him. No one wanted to, usually, because he was so entertaining. He was a bit annoyed at me for not taking a more active role in the general talk, and once urged me to assert myself. I did exactly that the next night. I talked and talked and Sherwood could not get a word in, much less an entire story. He was much more annoyed at me for doing that than for not participating enough.

After that, I stepped in only when I saw that Sherwood was going too far. He would get carried away at times and would actually scare some of the people that were there. A number of New Orleans debutantes visited us regularly and they were simply not accustomed to any man like Sherwood. He thought nothing of unbuttoning his shirt and grabbing one of them to dance with him. Once he had his shirt completely open and he made a wild dash at one of the girls. She dropped her purse, knocked over her chair and ran away in fright.

Sherwood was completely abashed by this, for of course he had only been having fun. I said: "Serves you right. Button up your shirt!"

There was a great deal of drinking among us but little drunkenness. We all seemed to feel that Prohibition was a personal affront and that we had a moral duty to undermine it. The great drink of the day was absinthe, which was even more illegal than whiskey because of the wormwood in it. Bill Spratling had bought ten large jugs of it from some woman whose bootlegger husband had died, and he shared his booty liberally with his friends. It was served over crushed ice, and since it did not have much taste of alcohol that way, it was consumed in quantities.

A lady reporter from the Midwest wanted to learn about the domestic side of Sherwood and she called me to arrange for an interview. I told her that Sherwood would probably be free that afternoon, but she said no, that she wanted to interview me. I was so surprised that I told her I would meet her in the Absinthe House, a famous speakeasy, instead of asking her into my home. We met, sipped absinthe, and later she reported to a presumably breathless and shocked Midwest audience: "Miss Elizabeth spends her days sipping absinthe in a popular New Orleans bistro." When I read the clipping I was outraged, but Sherwood was so gleeful about it that I finally had to treat it as a joke too.

Sherwood drank absinthe, but never cared what he drank or if he drank at all. He had the natural kind of high spirits that carried everyone along on the crest of his enthusiasms. But he thought of himself as a hard, two-fisted drinker because that is what he believed men should be.

I saw Sherwood drunk only once, after a party I had not attended. He came home and staggered noisily up the steps. I woke up immediately and sat up with great interest. "Why, Sherwood," I said, "I've never seen you drunk before. It'll be a new experience for me."

He looked at me rather owlishly for a long time, then he wheeled around and stumbled down the stairs again. I could hear him clattering around down there, knocking into things. Finally he came back up and slumped down on the bed, trying to get his shoes off. I was still watching him with great interest.

He sighed and looked at me. "Isn't this a fine example of how the world has gone to the dogs. If you were a good wife, you'd be mad at me for getting drunk."

I laughed and went back to sleep.

Not long after we moved to New Orleans, Sherwood's son Robert showed up. He had hitchhiked across the country to be with his father, but his father did not know quite what to do with him. Bob was around nineteen then and had never really been brought up at all. Cornelia was a fine mother, but found it hard to impose any discipline on her children and, of course, Sherwood had never even considered doing so.

Bob was a rather wild boy, gangling and awkward and dead sure that he was full grown and ready to join our friends as an equal. He seemed to think that because his father was a famous writer, he could write too.

Bob had been cool to me at first, but then he saw that all the young writers and artists liked me, so he decided to make an effort to be friendly. His initial overture consisted of showing me the stories he had written. I was willing enough to read them but I could not honestly praise them. He could neither spell nor punctuate and the stories seemed childish to me.

I tried to be tactful, but I did not want to pay for his friendship with a lie. "Bob, you know I think you'd better wait until you have something to say."

He did not understand that at all. He looked hurt and insisted on knowing what I meant. I said: "Bob, I'm much older than you are, you know, and maybe I'm just too old to be interested in your ideas. It's just not very meaningful to me. You still seem like a child to me."

He was somewhat put out about that, but still more

friendly than he had been before, which pleased me because it was difficult to have someone living in my house
who did not like me. At one point, Sherwood had come
to me and had said, "I wish you would do something
for me. Please be nicer to Bob."

"Well," I said, "You go to Bob first and tell him to
be nicer to me."

"You're just imagining that," Sherwood said.

"No, I'm not. He only puts up with me because there
are all those other people he likes coming around here."

For a while after that, Sherwood lavished affection
on the boy, talked to him at length, and gave him money
to spend as he pleased.

We both should have known that Bob would use
the money to get drunk. He wanted to be like the older
people in every way and the next time we saw the boy he
was so drunk that he could not stand.

It was too much for me to accept with equanimity.
"Sherwood," I said, "this can't go on. At his age, he
simply can't go out and get drunk like that."

Sherwood was furious with Bob, but it did no good
to rant and rave at him — he was barely conscious.
Sherwood worked himself into such a rage that he had
actually kicked the prostrate boy before I managed to
calm him down and get him to carry Bob up the long
narrow steps to his bedroom.

Though we never learned where Bob had bought the liquor, I was sure that none of our friends had given it to him. He adored Bill Spratling and Bill Faulkner and used any excuse he could devise to visit them, but I had specifically asked them not to give him anything to drink.

A while later I had a talk with Bob and told him, "When you're older, you'll just have to experiment until you know how much you can hold."

He was sheepish about the incident, and we established a sort of truce and got on well after that. Roark Bradford gave him a job on the *Times-Picayune*, but he was not disciplined enough to hold it for long. Finally, Bill Faulkner persuaded Sherwood and me to send Bob to the University of Virginia, where he could learn to dress properly and behave well with other people. Sherwood decided he could scrape together enough money and Bob was sent off to school.

Sherwood was deeply involved in writing a book he first wanted to call *Black Laughter* and then *Deep Laughter*. Then I suggested *Dark Laughter* to him and that is how it was published. Bill Faulkner was working on something he would not talk about. He patterned his days after Sherwood's, working in the morning and relaxing in the afternoons.

We took long strolls around the docks, watching the unhurried loading of the ships and breathing in the rich, changing aromas: the strange, musty smells of sacked sugar and the slightly burnt, nutty smell of coffee mingling with the wet, earthy aroma of fresh vegetables. Nearby was the French market, which was fascinating to us. At a certain hour of the day the market would be suddenly crowded with the grand ladies who had come with their servants to buy vegetables. All of them wore flowing, summery dresses and carried filmy parasols and flimsy wicker baskets into which they put nothing at all, for the baskets served only to indicate that the ladies had servants who carried things. They served no more practical function than the hats they wore. The ladies nodded to each other and chatted, while their maids trudged about buying crayfish and okra. It was a sheerly social spectacle and we loved it, but only as spectators. The ladies seemed almost afraid of anyone who actually lived in the Quarter.

In the evenings, Sherwood and Bill Faulkner sat around adding to and embroidering their rambling yarns about Al Jackson, a character they had invented between themselves, who herded sheep in the swamps. They had worked up a continuing saga about Al Jackson and his fantastic relatives, all of whom had webbed feet for swamp walking. It seemed to me that neither Sherwood nor Bill could be content with merely writing seriously during the day. At night they had to continue by making up bizarre tales that were actually parodies of the process of writing fiction. Later on, both writers were to use the Al Jackson stories: Faulkner in *Mosquitoes* and Sherwood in the country newspaper he bought.

One day Bill came to me and announced that he had finished writing a novel. Jokingly he added that he had observed Sherwood working only half days and that it seemed like a good way to make a living so he had tried it out for himself.

"Would you like Sherwood to read it?" I asked, for it was not at all unusual for writers to ask that of Sherwood.

"No," said Bill, "he's kind of busy with his own things right now."

I told Sherwood about this and he said that in return for the favor of not having to read the book he would recommend it to Horace Liveright, who was expected to visit us in New Orleans soon. He also said, more seriously, "Bill is one of them who will make it. He writes every day and is really serious about it. He knows what he is doing."

When Horace did come down, Sherwood met him on the street with a strikingly beautiful woman. That was nothing new. In New York, Horace was constantly seen with many beautiful women and had a widespread reputation for it.

Horace was a handsome man with dark and lively eyes and a pale skin. I had met him in New York and had not cared for him since I thought he was impossibly conceited, perhaps because of the many women who fell hopelessly in love with him. He seemed to have a new girl every six months, and every six months his apartment was completely redecorated by the latest girl. When I knew him, his place was totally black — black upholstery, black mirrors, black glass over everything. It was all very expensive and, I thought, quite dreadful. Horace was a daredevil who would try anything. It earned him a meteoric reputation in the publishing world, but when he applied the same daring to the stock market he went broke. He had always struck me as the kind of man who likes to take hold of your hand, under the table.

In New Orleans, when Sherwood saw him with yet another girl, Horace said, "Meet my wife."

Without thinking, Sherwood said, "Oh yeah?"

It turned out that the woman really was Horace's wife, and the chance encounter was a bit stilted from that moment on. But of course Horace forgave Sherwood and they had many talks together.

At that time, Ben Huebsch was Sherwood's publisher. Ben was a dear, sweet, fat, old Jewish man, rather bumbling. He had accepted Sherwood's books when no one else would, and there was a deep loyalty between the two men. But Ben was not really much of a businessman and had so little capital that he could not afford to properly publicize his authors. Sherwood had made very little money from his books, and by this time he was beginning to suspect that he might do better with some other publisher.

Horace invited us to Antoine's restaurant to talk over the situation. It was our favorite place and certainly the finest eating spot in all of New Orleans. Now, I believe there are long lines of people waiting to get in, but in those days there was no problem. The main part of the restaurant was a large, plain room with high fans describing lazy circles in the air. The floors were tiled and gleaming clean. The panels of mirrors around the walls made the place look even bigger and plainer. The elegance of Antoine's lay not in its decor but in the cuisine that was created there.

There were a number of private rooms, some very ornate and Victorian, but Sherwood always favored the plain, unadorned one with a single round table covered with a white tablecloth. In its center sat an old-fashioned carafe of ice water. We ordered oysters Rockefeller, for they had been invented there, and then turned to the weighty decision of the main course. I settled for shrimp in aspic.

When we had finished off the meal with *café brûlot,* Horace was finally ready to talk business. Sherwood admitted that he was becoming discouraged by the way his books were selling with Ben Huebsch, but added that he was very fond of the man.

Horace nodded understandingly, for everyone liked Huebsch. It was impossible not to, and I knew that Sherwood was suffering guilt feelings for thinking about going to another publisher.

Horace Liveright was acquiring most of the better writers of the time by the simple method of offering them more money than any other publisher. It is, I think, an expedient that is still used today. Now, Horace made a proposal that was, for those days, both startling and generous. He offered to send Sherwood a hundred dollars a week and he would expect to receive in return about one book a year. He was very confident that he could sell Sherwood's books in a way that would make money for both of them.

Sherwood did not have to mull it over very long. For the first time he would be free of money worries and be able to concentrate completely on writing. He told Horace that he had just finished a book called *Dark Laughter* and that Horace could publish it. It was to become Sherwood's only best seller.

A book named *Soldier's Pay* was also handed over

to Horace and he later agreed to publish that too. But at the time, we had no idea what would happen to Bill Faulkner's novel. Horace took it off to New York with him and life returned to normal in the Quarter.

Not long after that, another group of Northerners came down to see us. For once, Bill Faulkner had taken control of the conversation and was talking very earnestly for a long time to the visitors. I was out in the kitchen getting something together to eat, and I could hear him dimly but could not make out the actual words. Finally I came out and listened to him. He was seriously propounding a theory that white people should not mate with colored people because, like the mule offspring of a donkey and a horse, the resultant mulattos could not bear children.

I looked at him in astonishment, not quite sure that he was pulling the legs of his audience. "Why, Bill Faulkner," I said, "I had always been told that was the way you crossed over the line and got to be white."

For a moment he was shocked, then he burst into laughter. Bill and I never talked about his true feeling for Negroes, but in his later books he wrote of the ambivalent feelings of love and guilt and fear that the South harbors for the once enslaved race.

Bill was often difficult at parties. He loved to put things over on people and sometimes his audience never would realize they had been duped. He was also very sure of his own knowledge about certain things and was flatly outspoken about saying so.

We were being visited by Ferdinand Schevill at one time. Ferdinand taught history at the University of Chicago and had written a book on Greek and Roman history that was being used in schools all over the world. He was a very close friend, but he was a staunchly conservative man who probably thought we were all a bit mad in New Orleans. He liked me because I was quiet, but I knew he was startled by the free-wheeling talk and easy laughter of our friends.

Bill Faulkner set off upon one of his more improbable expositions, touching on an area in which Ferdinand was expert. Ferdinand corrected him, perhaps somewhat pedantically. Bill had been eyeing Ferdinand suspiciously because he distrusted anyone he regarded as stuffy or as a "philistine." Bill lashed out with some insulting retort to poor Ferdinand, who did not know how to react. It was not the kind of thing that ever happened to him in his academic world.

Bill had a wide range of knowledge, not all of it based on fact. Tonight he was clearly mistaken, but even if he had been accurate, I would have been angry at him for having insulted our guest, and for having been rude to an older man.

101

But it was too leisurely a life for anyone to long remain angry with anyone. Even Sherwood was not upset when Bill Spratling drew a number of caricatures of all the people in the Quarter and Bill Faulkner wrote an introduction for it that was a parody of Sherwood's style. They published the little book as *Sherwood Anderson and Other Famous Creoles* and brought it to Sherwood. He looked at it and stated flatly, "It isn't very funny."

Some of the biographers of Sherwood have made a great deal of that incident, saying that he never spoke to Bill Faulkner again because he had been so grievously wounded by the parody. Actually, Sherwood had forgotten all about it in a short time, and no one was radically affected by it in any way. Sherwood and Bill remained friendly until Bill left for Europe and they wrote to each other from time to time after that.

Sherwood did have a brief quarrel with Hamilton Basso, but that too soon evaporated. He and Ham had always enjoyed talking about writing, which is not always a good idea for two writers. At any rate, Ham wrote a story which was very similar to one that Sherwood had recently written. He came to our place and showed it to Sherwood, who immediately said, "Why, that's my story. You've taken one of my ideas for a story."

"Let him have it, Sherwood." I said, "You've always got plenty of ideas for stories."

But Sherwood had already written his own version of the story and was annoyed at Ham. He was very good at getting rid of anyone he did not like at the moment. He simply became disagreeable to the person in disfavor. Ham was sensitive enough to get the idea immediately and did not come around for a while. But the argument was soon forgotten. We all had such an easy and pleasant relationship that the slightest discordance created unreasonably hurt feelings.

Sherwood went on lecture tours to supplement his income, but I went with him only once, to Chicago. I wanted to see Clara and Ferdinand Schevill again and I was curious about how Sherwood's audience responded to him. I did not care for the lectures myself, but the people who attended such affairs seemed to love them and women flocked around him adoringly when they were over. He had memorized several different talks, such as "The Modern Writer" and "America — The Storehouse of Vitality," and I thought his style was quite wooden. But his reputation as a wild man had preceded him and the audiences sat in rapt attention waiting for him to say something shocking. He rarely ever did, though, unless some little old lady asked him an especially stupid question. Then he would become quite testy.

After that one trip I stayed home while Sherwood was off on his tours. There were always domestic problems to be coped with. We had a Negro cook named Josephine and she provided us with diversions as well as dinner. Like many Negroes in New Orleans, she was not at all like the Negroes in the rest of the South. She was lighter-skinned, with freckles, and her hair was reddish. She was very proud and could be arrogant when it pleased her. She constructed rich, complicated Creole dishes for us, but told me she herself ate chitlings and cooked turnip greens at home.

Josephine had once been the head nutcracker in a pecan factory, which meant that she was skilled at cracking the pecans so the meat would not be broken. She had a "gen'mun" friend, as she called him. He was still working at the pecan factory and it seemed that proximity and convenience caused him to take up with another girl. Josephine stood up for her rights by stabbing the other girl and she was jailed for it.

Sherwood was away at the time and I had no idea what to do about the matter. Hamilton Basso kindly filled me in on the procedure. I would have to bail poor Josephine out; it was done all the time. He said he would go along with me and I was glad to accept his offer. I had no idea what I might find in a Night Court.

Ham had asked some of his friends and had learned that on the night we were to appear in court, there would be a "cross" judge. Everyone knew the judges —

both their schedules and their temperaments — and they would try to appear only before the more benign ones. As it happened, our luck was bad.

Night Court was a sprawling, ugly building, made more depressing by the people who wandered in its echoing gray halls and by the lurking odors of stale sweat that seemed to have permeated the concrete walls.

The judge proved to be "cross" indeed. When Josephine came up before him, he did not even bother to question her about her story, as though she were incapable of coherent reply. Instead, he demanded to know if I could vouch for her character.

I was irritated by his manner, so I answered in the same curt tone he had used to me. "I don't know what you mean by 'vouching.' She's my cook and she's a very good one."

"What about her character?" the judge asked peevishly.

"She's very good when she's with me. I don't know what she does at night. I don't see her. She goes home."

The judge glared at me and for a moment I thought he might send us both off to jail, but then he shrugged. "Oh take her off. Pay ten dollars and take her off."

I paid the money and we hustled Josephine out of Night Court. She was not markedly grateful; it was something of a fringe benefit that she expected from her "white folks." At that time, Negroes sometimes fought and "cut" each other and nothing much was made of it. Josephine had simply avenged herself and her honor and now she could forget all about it.

 six

Even with Sherwood's new source of income from Horace Liveright, I felt we could use more money, so I looked around for something to do. Lucille and Marc Antony were close friends of ours and I knew that they were short of money too. Lucille came from a very wealthy Jewish family but had quarreled with her mother, Mrs. Gottschalk, and had run off to Paris to live with Marc Antony. When they both returned to New Orleans, she was completely cut off from the family fortune. Lucille and I got together one day and decided it would be fun to open a decorating shop.

Neither of us had a head for business and the shop was run along languid, leisurely lines. It became a gathering ground for our friends and we never did make any money — only new friends.

Anita Loos came into the shop to see me one day and was completely dismayed by the situation. "I never saw a shop run like this before in my life," she announced.

"We don't really think of it as a business," I said, somewhat defensively. "We just have fun here and once in a while we sell something."

Anita looked about for a while longer, then said, "This is a silly way to waste your time."

By that time Anita had written literally hundreds of screenplays in Hollywood and I think she simply did not understand the slower tempo of life in New Orleans. She had come to New Orleans because she needed a rest from her husband, John Emerson, who was a volatile and demanding individual. She stayed at the St. Charles Hotel and worked very hard, just as she played very hard. She was writing *Gentlemen Prefer Blondes* then, and her system was to write part of it each week and send it off to her publisher without fail.

Anita was a wonderful-looking girl, so little and cunning and smart. She would not talk about the book she was writing with anybody, but she was a part of the writing crowd and we all adored her. She had been one of the first to rebel against the long hair that was then fashionable, and had cut her dark black hair into a boyish bob, with wispy tendrils forming bangs. With anyone but Anita, the hair style might have been shocking, but she was able to get away with anything. She wore flamboyant clothes with great style and the sparkle of her wit and ways delighted us all.

Anita was about half Sherwood's size and she called him "Swatty" with pert impudence that he loved, but only from her. Young men flocked in droves from all over New Orleans when the word got around that she was there. She was so gay and amusing that it was hard to believe she was also a dedicated, serious worker.

Anita's writing was rigidly separated from her partying, and I imagine that was why she was perturbed by the relaxed blend of business and pleasure in our decorating shop. The shop did not last very long anyway, for Lucille managed to somehow effect a reconciliation with her mother, Mrs. Gottschalk, and for a time, she and Marc actually lived with her family.

Marc's fifteen-year-old brother was also living in the house and he was a trial for everyone. He was behaving very badly for fifteen-year-old reasons of his own and Marc was very concerned about him. His father was dead and it was Marc's responsibility to bring the boy up properly. If Marc had been a more imposing figure of a man, it might have been easier. But he was a slight person who looked not far from adolescence himself, and his younger brother resented his position of authority.

It is possible that Sherwood identified the boy with his own son Robert, because he was highly sympathetic toward him and agreed that he was being ill-treated. In a burst of quite typical generosity, Sherwood told the boy he could live in the room that Robert used when he visited. Sherwood did not consult with me about this, and before I knew it, Marc's brother had moved into the attic room.

Marc came over to talk to me privately. He was very upset about the situation, but did not want to anger Sherwood or lose his friendship. "Elizabeth, can you tell Sherwood that the boy is my responsibility and I can't have my little brother staying anyplace away from my house. He has to be living with us."

By then I had figured out what had happened. Sherwood had been overwhelmed by another swift seizure of sympathy and had recklessly offered the boy sanctuary without thinking of the consequences.

"You know how Sherwood is," I told Marc. "He didn't mean to hurt your feelings or interfere with your family. He just wanted to help the boy and thought this was the best way to do it. Don't worry about it though: I'll talk to Sherwood."

I did. Sherwood was surprised that Marc was upset,

but after thinking it through, he agreed that he had acted hastily. He had a long talk with the boy, after which he was returned to the Antony fold.

Sherwood was an unpredictable man to live with, even apart from his occasional spurts of rashness. A writer is an actor who must play many roles in the theater of his fiction and Sherwood was never able to confine his role-playing to his prose. He adopted different personalities wholeheartedly and, I think, unconsciously.

I was never sure who Sherwood would be when he woke in the morning. If he was a Millionaire he would be quite capable of going out and planking down hard cash for whatever fed his fancy. At such times he was expansive, confident and bold. These were his "party" times.

But the next morning he might be the Poor Man who had to work hard for a living, and he would go out and dig furiously in the garden, then come in and go at his writing just as furiously.

It was difficult to keep track of his moods, but I was expected to join in them and play the same part. When he was a Millionaire I had to put on my best clothes and help him spend money. He took me by complete surprise one day when I was wearing a dark maroon gingham dress I had made myself. He was peevish as he informed me: "You're not a farmer's wife, you know."

Some time later, when we were in Paris, I bought some clothes that were expensive. One of the dresses was black lace with a red chiffon lining and a pink sheath beneath that. I modeled it for Sherwood, who was interested in some detail on it that he liked. After a while he grew thoughtful. "Where did you get that?" he asked finally.

"Chanel's," I said.

"You know you can't afford clothes like that," he said.

"Well, I bought it and paid for it. What do you mean?"

It was true that I had paid for it with my own money, so he decided to change the course of the argument. "You're an American. You shouldn't try to rig yourself up as a Parisienne."

"Why not?"

"American women should dress more simply and leave the French clothes to the French women," he said, shrugging.

"That's not true," I protested. "These shops couldn't even stay open if it weren't for Americans buying their clothes. They couldn't live on just what the French buy themselves."

It was a new idea for him and he was always receptive to that. "That's true enough," he admitted and went back to his usual attitude of not noticing what I wore.

In New Orleans, Sherwood acquired a number of new roles that he enjoyed playing. He could be a struggling, poor writer at one time and then the grand old man of letters at another. He could be the simple, honest American workingman who insisted on having at every meal "brown, white and green" — meat, potato and vegetable — with no fancy asides, and then later pride himself on being a polished connoisseur of world cuisine at the restaurants we went to. None of this was thought out by him; it was simply that whatever he did, he did thoroughly.

He wrote swiftly and seemingly without effort, then went back over his manuscripts and weeded out the parts he no longer liked. Because of his revisions and diligent pruning and rewriting, the end result was that he worked almost as hard as those other writers, such as Hemingway, who labored mightily over every phrase.

He liked people to believe that he wrote *"con amore,"* with the prose flowing from his mind naturally and fluidly. He pretended to have little regard for "technique" as such, but from his many talks with other writers, I knew how deeply involved he was with the mechanics of his craft.

Sherwood had a natural ear for dialect and often adopted in his own speech the terrible clichés used by the kind of people he wrote about. I used to laugh at these lapses and he would appear to be hurt, but then laugh as he realized that he had sounded exactly like that terrible President Harding. Harding would make speeches that were simply riddled with clichés and cozy homilies that were deadly. People became so ashamed that he was the President they would be unable to listen to him.

I also read Sherwood's manuscripts to catch any glaring clichés he had not already deleted himself, and to correct the spelling, which was ludicrous. He had hired a typist at one time, but her spelling was, if anything, inferior to his.

In New Orleans, Sherwood was no longer writing short stories, but concentrating on his books, which seemed unfortunate to me, because I thought his best writing came in short spurts of creativity. He could neither sustain a mood in his prose nor in his person. Even his *Winesburg, Ohio* was a collection of short pieces with a central theme. In some of his novels, there would be stretches of dull dry prose, then suddenly there would be a short passage that was so brilliant that he could be forgiven all the rest of it.

Though I never told him so, I had a strange feeling about the women in his fiction. Sherwood always believed he was writing about women who were charming and attractive and witty, but to me they all seemed like rather dull country girls. I do not think that Sherwood ever understood much about women and certainly he preferred the social companionship of men, whom he could talk to as boisterously as he pleased and say whatever occurred to him. But then, no one ever understood everything about Sherwood Anderson. Certainly, I did not.

Perhaps Sherwood's main contribution to literature was the influence he had on the younger writers he knew. He was convinced that writers should look to their own roots for inspiration and he expressed this conviction many times to Bill Faulkner. Sherwood wrote of the odd, inner loneliness that is peculiar to the Midwest, and Bill later began to write about the convoluted, incestuous world of the South.

New Orleans was acquiring a certain fame as a "bohemian" literary center, and a good many writers came down to visit us and to exchange ideas. Carl Sandburg proved to be just as accomplished at storytelling as Sherwood. He would entertain our group with long tales of things that had happened to him, embellishing and embroidering along the way. All our friends knew his books and poetry and we had long, leisurely evenings outside on our patio, with the warm wind rustling the palm trees and providing a beguiling background when Sandburg strummed his guitar, his long, yellow-white hair like a nimbus around his rugged face.

They were full, rich nights, with ideas flashing like fireflies and phrases rippling like spontaneous poetry. Sherwood was actively interested in Sandburg because of their mutual interest in the Civil War and Lincoln. Sherwood had wanted to write a book about Abraham Lincoln and had actually started working on one, but, of course, Sandburg did it first. Both Sherwood and Sandburg were Northerners and the Southern writers we knew had their own views of the Civil War. With Lyle Saxon, Roark Bradford and Bill Faulkner adding their ideas to the discussion, things became fairly spirited at times.

The first time I talked to Carl Sandburg, I was forced into a situation in which I had to admit I had not read any of his books. I had tried to steer the conversation so the subject would not come up, but he asked me about some specific point in one of his books and I had to confess. "Well," he said, after a decidedly awkward pause, "at least you're honest about it." I had read his poetry though, so my faux pas was not final.

Edmund Wilson showed up in New Orleans and brought us all up to date on what was going on in New York and what our friends were currently up to. Edmund had the kind of brilliantly educated mind that could not be bothered with the ordinary mechanics of everyday living. He was totally impractical and had no idea how to do such things as send his clothes to the cleaners or cook a meal. He was accustomed to having someone around who took care of such matters for him. He had a secretary who did everything for him, even in those days. Somehow, he had been trusted to come to New Orleans alone, and he seemed surprised and rather pleased that he had managed to get there. His typewriter was not working and one day he wandered off to have it repaired. He returned, proud of himself for having found a repair shop and then having found his way back. A few days later he decided the machine would be ready, so he started out of the house to pick it up. Suddenly he stopped and stood in the doorway for a moment with his back turned to us, obviously lost in thought. Finally he turned around and helplessly confessed that he had no idea where he had left his typewriter or what the name of the shop was. He spent the entire afternoon tracking through the Quarter for the repair shop.

Around that time, Sherwood discovered that he had a little extra money from the sale of *Dark Laughter.* Typically, he decided to spend as much of it as he could. Anita Loos was still working away on *Gentlemen Prefer Blondes*, so Sherwood wanted to entertain her by hiring a yacht for a brief excursion out on Lake Pontchartrain. He arranged the whole affair and asked a number of his friends, then mentioned the trip to Anita. She apologized prettily, but said she would not be able to make it. She had a deadline and had to keep working at her book so she would have enough material to mail off on Saturday. I never knew whether it was a psychological deadline she set for herself or whether her publisher actually demanded a certain amount of wordage each week.

But the party was set to go and it did. Ham Basso came, with a giddy young girl. Bill Faulkner, Bill Spratling, Lillian Marcus Friend, and Marc and Lucille Antony were all on board, as were several young girls Sherwood had casually asked along. The captain of the boat was a professional sailor who seemed greatly amused by his motley load of passengers. It was a very adventurous thing to do, or so we all thought. We sailed off without the slightest idea about where we were going or what we would find.

The first thing we found was bad weather, neither wet enough to storm and rage dramatically nor dry enough to create a mysterious Jack London fog. It simply drizzled and provided neither excitement nor allure.

I sat inside apprehensively for hours, waiting for great surges of nausea to come over me, which usually happened to me at sea. When it became apparent that nothing of the sort was going to happen, I relaxed enough to take a look around. No one else was seasick either, which was an unexpected bonus. Lake Pontchartrain was large enough so that no land was visible from the boat, only a quietly billowing mass of gray sea, pockmarked by occasional sprays of rain.

We were out for two days and it struck me that we might as well have remained at home, for we all sat around the galley talking, just as we did every night on our patio. The only real difference was the food, which was bad.

Bill Faulkner later wrote *Mosquitoes*, a novel loosely based on our modest excursion which he fictionally enlivened with several love affairs and violent personality clashes. Most of the people in our group were satirized in the book.

Lillian Marcus Friend, who owned the *Double-Dealer*, came from a distinguished Jewish family in New Orleans and had a birdlike face in which everything came to a point. Whenever I talked to her I half expected her to peck at me. I did not get along particularly well with her. She considered herself to be a social and literary arbiter and did not care to be challenged or corrected. She had been divorced and lived, with her two sons, at her family's house. She had more or less adopted Sherwood when he had lived alone in New Orleans for a year, and she insisted on being the center of contention at all times. She enjoyed arguing and would often oppose an idea simply to stir up controversy.

In *Mosquitoes*, Bill satirized Lillian as Mrs. Maurier, a raging, culture-bent dowager who lived only to surround herself with famous names and who was characterized mostly by silliness. It was probably the cruelest cut of all.

Sherwood was portrayed in the book as Dawson Fairchild, and it was a gentle, kindly caricature of a famous author who has a tendency to pontificate and who is somewhat awed by erudition and sophistication. But Dawson Fairchild is perhaps the most sympathetic character in the book, so Sherwood did not fare too badly.

Bill Spratling was depicted as a poet named Mark Frost who groans audibly each time Dawson Fairchild goes into another long spiel about Al Jackson, the swamp sheepherder.

All the giddy young girls were unceremoniously lumped together and immortalized as a character named Jenny Steinbauer. Even the dreary food was satirized in Bill's book. He doomed his characters to a steady diet of nothing but grapefruit, with Mrs. Maurier (Lillian Friend) constantly insisting, "But they say it's impossible to get tired of it."

The actual trip, however, was quite uneventful. We

took the yacht to Covington, across the lake, sailed around aimlessly for a time, then returned. No one was greatly agitated or depressed by the experience. We all enjoyed each other's company and it was simply an extension of our usual gatherings under nautical circumstances. Some of us may have been secretly disappointed that nothing more flamboyant did happen.

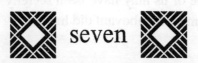 seven

Weeks Hall was a strange and tragic person in New Orleans. Sherwood once wrote that Weeks had a better painter's mind and feeling than anyone around but that he had been so twisted by life he was unable to do anything healthy. He had gone to art school and had been considered the most promising of all the students. He developed a fine painting technique, but was unable to paint. He would start a canvas and paint a picture, then paint the same picture over it with a few minor changes, and this would go on and on. He would spend years on a painting, unable to stop or to start on something new.

Weeks had been dominated in his early years by a wealthy old aunt named Mrs. Torrion, who was interested only in food. She had lavished little attention on her young ward and now that he was grown she dismissed him entirely. Weeks lived in a hovel and had no money at all, but Mrs. Torrion offered him nothing but occasional invitations to sumptuous dinners.

Sherwood and I were invited to several such dinners and they were staggering. They began with a bout of drinking that was intensive and long-lasting. Whenever I was asked to one of Mrs. Torrion's affairs, I would eat a banana before leaving the house, for fear that I would be forced to drink so much I might get drunk.

The Torrion dinners held an odd fascination for both Sherwood and myself because they were such obsessive occasions. The instant we entered the house we were handed a Sazerac cocktail, which is a drink made by stirring together a jigger of bourbon with a half-jigger of vermouth and a dash of bitters and orange bitters. This is stirred into crushed ice, then poured out into a heavy, chilled tumbler with a few drops of absinthe.

Mrs. Torrion was a crisp and rigid old woman with crisp gray hair that looked as though it might have been ironed into place. She presided over her salon as if it were a courtroom and I should not have been at all surprised had she appeared with a gavel. Sazerac cocktails were pressed upon us regularly — one did not dare refuse — until Mrs. Torrion decided it was time to dine.

The dinner would invariably be an orgy of superb Creole cooking, starting, perhaps, with delicately flavored fish in a broth of tomatoes, peppers, parsley, thyme, saffron, olive oil, garlic and white wine. Then, if crayfish were in season, they would be brought out in high style on steaming platters. After that, perhaps a sweetbread omelette and then a plate of baked red snapper in Creole sauce that had been cooked in wine. Then a salad, and then the pièce de résistance, a *daube glacé,* which is a jellied meat with pepper, bay leaf, cloves and countless other spices. It was a dark brown, lovely dish, both in appearance and taste. All this, of course, was accompanied by a steady procession of different wines.

Mrs. Torrion would eat and eat, long after everyone else could do nothing more than halfheartedly push food around on their plates, too sated to even pretend to unabated enthusiasm. She ate with tremendous gusto and style and her appetite never seemed to be diminished or even affected by the amount of food she consumed, working with the precision of a surgeon as she deftly cut the food into morsels and popped each bit into her mouth with never a flaw in her manners. It was an awesome sight.

The final touch of the meal was, almost incongruously, a simple cheese or a peach, followed by coffee laced with brandy. It was late at night before anyone could leave the table, and it was with considerable difficulty that we did so, even then.

I had never before known anyone who was so single-mindedly dedicated to food as Mrs. Torrion. She did her own shopping, cruising through the open markets with all her senses attuned for flaws in the crayfish or bruised turtle eggs. It took up most of her morning and the rest of the day was devoted to overseeing the complicated cooking processes.

Poor Weeks ate almost nothing at all except for these odd orgies to which he would sometimes be invited. He could rarely force down more than two courses, because his appetite and capacity had shrunk in the interim since the last dinner invitation.

Weeks was a slight man with none of the wiriness of many small men; he had a curious soft quality that looked, somehow, unformed. From beneath black bangs, his narrow cat's eyes stared out at a world he could not fathom. He was an unpredictable creature who would get blindly drunk and start fights with men twice his size or insult women in bars. Everyone was afraid of what he would do next and what would happen to him as a consequence of it.

Then, someone in his extensive family died and left Weeks an unexpected fortune. This is the sort of thing that seems to happen only in the South. A person may not have heard or thought of a distant relative in years, then suddenly finds himself the heir to that person's money. It happened to Weeks and his life was changed, but not, perhaps, improved.

Weeks indulged himself in his great nostalgia for the romantic Southern past by buying a lovely old plantation house on the Teche River and restoring it exactly as it had been in the days of its splendor. He spent most of the inherited fortune in buying and reconstructing this house, and it was an impressive, if chilling, masterpiece. Bill Spratling caricatured Weeks in *Sherwood Anderson and Other Famous Creoles* as "Baron Teche" or "Weeks Hall by Moonlight."

Sherwood and I were invited to spend a weekend at Weeks's plantation, and mostly out of curiosity we accepted. The house had four great white pillars rising from the lower balcony and then on up to the towering roof. Both balconies were enclosed by beautifully wrought iron railings with a lacy fragility that contrasted with the massive pillars.

The garden around the house was flawlessly kept, with an emerald-green lawn and artfully sculptured shrubbery. There were an old-fashioned marble angel and many cupids posted about the garden.

Inside the house, everything was antebellum. Just inside the entrance, a stairway curved with stately grace

126

to the upper floors and a finely carved archway led into the salon. Weeks had great taste and artistry and had been scrupulous about recapturing the exact atmosphere, even to the point of excluding electricity from the house. The whole place was lighted with lamps and candles. Also, he had dismissed from his mind such modern innovations as window and door screens, and the mosquitoes from the swamps around the Bayou Teche buzzed and hummed freely in the house.

The night we spent in the house was eerie, with the flickering light of candles casting shadows that writhed in dark corners. Outside, there were the electric murmuring of katydids and the low, grumbling "knee-deep" of frogs. The sound seemed to come in waves. Suddenly it would cease and we could hear only the distant, muted river chuckling sluggishly along.

Many times in my own house I would go off and leave Sherwood to talk far into the night with his friends. This night, however, I stayed up, unable to steel myself to venture into the dimly lit upper reaches of the house. At one point Sherwood asked me if I would like to see the garden by moonlight. I simply looked at him as if he had gone mad and he hastily changed the subject.

Weeks Hall lived alone in that huge house except for one man, a tyrannical old Negro servant who dominated Weeks. It was obvious to both Sherwood and myself that

Weeks was terrified of the servant, who ordered him about constantly. It was a strange, depressing relationship I could not understand.

Sherwood loved the house and spent hours roaming about, exploring it. He did not even seem to mind the mosquitoes, which were plaguing me. I developed a kind of horror of the place and was vastly relieved when the weekend finally ended. It all seemed to me very much like Bill Faulkner's later novels. There was something terribly wrong in that reliquary of the past and it was something that was neither visible nor audible.

When we were back in our own home in New Orleans, I began to realize that Sherwood was becoming restless with his life in the Quarter. The summer had been oppressively hot and I was sure he would not endure another like it. We went on a short excursion to Marion, Virginia, and looked over the country. Sherwood was greatly taken with the rustic setting, but I was not certain how I would fare as a country wife. When we returned to New Orleans, we began talking about leaving that city to avoid another sweltering summer.

Our cook, Josephine, interrupted one such conversation by telling us that she would have to go to Baton Rouge to attend her brother's funeral. We told her how sorry we were to hear of her brother's death, and gave her the money she would need to get there and back. We would miss her and her fine cooking but of course we understood that she would have to go.

For the next few days we heard nothing of Josephine, then we began receiving postcards from her, letting us know the progress of the funeral and what followed.

In a week she was back with two little children, as thin as squirrels and ragged as street urchins. They were orphans, Josephine told me. Her brother's wife had died some time ago, and now that her brother was gone, the two children were all alone in the world and Christmas was coming on. Clearly, we would have to do something for the children and give them some kind of Christmas.

We had hired another cook to replace Josephine while she was gone and the substitute did not like the prospect of being jobless again. We kept her on for a while, so that Josephine could get settled with her two little orphans. Finally the substitute cook saw us giving Josephine a number of things for the children and she came to me indignantly.

"Miz Anderson," she said, "that woman ain't got no brother and he ain't dead. And them ain't his kids."

"What on earth do you mean?" I asked.

"She never went to no Baton Rouge. She got some friends there to mail off them postcards. That woman just wants to make the most out of you and then get out herself. She picked up them kids off the street."

129

"But Josephine likes it here," I said, much dismayed. "Why would she want to get out?"

"She heard you talking about going away somewhere. I heard it too. She just wants to get all she can out of you while you're still here."

It was true. I looked into the matter discreetly, I thought, but there is no such thing as discretion with the great, omni-encompassing grapevine of the servant world in New Orleans. Josephine heard that I was onto her tricks and quickly disappeared, sending the two "orphans" back to the family from whom she had borrowed them.

It was time, we decided, to get out of New Orleans. Not because of Josephine, of course, but it seemed one more indication that it was a good idea for us to leave. Sherwood was slowly sinking into one of those deep, black depressions I came to know so well later. *Dark Laughter* had been a best seller, but many critics had attacked it, and Ernest Hemingway had just written and published *The Torrents of Spring*, a savage, slashing satire on Sherwood's prose style.

It had been a petty, cruel thing for Hemingway to do and I was never able to forgive him for it, or for the letter he subsequently sent to Sherwood. In his letter, Hemingway wrote of *The Torrents of Spring* as if it had been a fatal blow to Sherwood as a writer. He said he had written it in six weeks, on a sudden impulse, and that it was intended to put an end to the idea that there was anything valuable in Sherwood's writing. It was a repellently patronizing letter that spoke in sports terms of the "knock-out blow" he had delivered to Sherwood.

The truth of the matter, it later developed, was that Scott Fitzgerald wanted Hemingway to leave Horace Liveright and change to Fitzgerald's own publisher, much the same way that small boys want their best friends to be on their team. The way to do it, Fitzgerald suggested, was to write something that would be completely unacceptable to Horace Liveright. That would void the contract with him. Since Sherwood was Horace's star writer at that time, a savage attack on him in the form of *The Torrents of Spring* would be turned down by him. So Hemingway wrote the childishly insulting book and handed it to Horace, who was shocked by it and torn between his loyalty to both writers. Finally he had to stay with Sherwood and he allowed Hemingway to go to another publisher.

The same thing could have been accomplished if Hemingway had mustered up enough nerve to simply tell Horace that he wished to change publishers. Instead, Hemingway chose to turn on Sherwood, who had been responsible for having his first book published. Hemingway had once sat at Sherwood's feet in Chicago, absorbing many of his prose techniques and philosophical concepts. Now, in a kind of Oedipal father-slaying he had savaged his former mentor as he would later do to Gertrude Stein and, indeed, Fitzgerald himself, in *A Moveable Feast*. It reminded me of the man who said about his enemy, "Why does he hate me so? I've never done anything for him."

Sherwood responded to Hemingway's insufferable letter by writing back: "My books will last longer than yours will. Don't get too uppity."

All of this unfortunately happened at a time when Sherwood was beginning to have doubts about his writing. The act of writing had always been natural for him, and now the process had become torturous. He wondered if he had written himself out, exhausted all his themes.

Sherwood had always been an advocate of the "geographical cure" and now I too hoped that moving to another scene would renew him and his self-confidence. But the wanderer was fated to find only the other side of the mountain, never Nirvana.

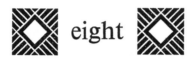 eight

We spent the summer of 1925 in Troutdale, Virginia, in the farmhouse of the John Greear family, while Sherwood worked on his next book, *Tar — a Midwest Childhood*. It cost only two dollars a day for board, room, laundry and mending. The Greears were amiable, hospitable people with five sons: David, Philip, Solomon, John and Joshua, all of whom adored Sherwood. He would work on *Tar* for a few hours each morning, then would play horseshoes with the boys or sit around the kitchen table playing "Flinch." If the boys went off on a possum hunt, Sherwood would be right there among them, as enthusiastic as the youngest of the boys.

When Sherwood, in his exploratory wanderings,

came upon a small cabin in the middle of a cornfield, the Greear boys obligingly swept out the accumulated dust and built him a crude table on which to write. Sherwood had become obsessed with the corn and the living things that surrounded him. He confessed to me that at times he would run outside the cabin and read chapters of *Tar* aloud to the cornfield. It may have saved his life. Some time later, after we became known around the countryside, one of the mountain men said they had sent someone crawling through the cornfield toward the little cabin to spy on Sherwood, because they thought he was a revenuer. When they heard him orating to the cornstalks, they concluded that, instead, he was merely crazy.

I was not as comfortable with the Greear family as was Sherwood. I was accustomed to having a house of my own, and though the Greears were intelligent, we had little in common. They lived in a near complete cultural vacuum and had nothing to think about but the exigencies of farm life.

I suggested to Sherwood that we might live in a slightly larger town, but by that time he had made up his mind that he would settle down and live in this area. He rented an old horse and older buggy and went meandering along the dirt roads that led through the mountains, thus increasing the sharp suspicions of the mountaineers, all of whom were involved in the zealous production of quantities of corn liquor. On one of his rambling excursions he followed a winding road that ran next to a brook and came to a small valley nestled among the hills. There he saw a small farm and met the widow who owned it. She was trudging down the road with a huge brass kettle balanced on her head. He stopped her and asked if she wanted to sell her farm. She instantly replied that she did, because she wanted to move back home to Georgia. Sherwood bought the place on the spot, without a word to me.

I was frankly apprehensive as we drove out to look at it, but Sherwood's high spirits were contagious as always, and the countryside was undeniably beautiful. There was an old orchard going to seed but still reclaimable, wild fruit and fragrant flowers. The hills were quilt-worked with purple rhododendrons and the yellow of a high and lovely flowering bush.

We moved into the old farmhouse and settled into our roles, myself as country wife and Sherwood as the Squire. Sherwood had the ancient, tottering barn torn down and carted away, and beneath it he found richly fertilized soil. At once he set about planting an unreasonable amount of zinnias and went about proclaiming himself the Zinnia King of Grayson County.

When I acquired a flock of turkeys, he promptly

dubbed me the Turkey Queen of the same county. He was scornful of the turkeys, however, and would have nothing to do with them. But turkeys proved to be practically no trouble at all to raise. As they grow up, they go pecking in the fields, eating grasshoppers and insects and generally helping the crops. The little turkeys were more troublesome, for they tend to die off if their feet get even slightly wet and our kitchen was continually cluttered with little turkeys getting their feet wiped. Sherwood, of course, refused to set foot in the kitchen.

I sent off to Montgomery Ward for wire netting to make turkey pens and they shipped me a roll of netting that was only about ten inches high. It did not seem to make any difference, for the turkeys never learned how to jump over it. It was enough for them to know that the barrier was there and they never crossed it, except on one shattering occasion. The turkeys were handsome birds, white, with brown tips on their feathers, and they were identical in appearance to the wild turkeys in the vicinity. One day a wild turkey took an interest in his captive cousins and came flying in to investigate. My turkeys had never seen one of their own fly before. I suppose it had just never occurred to them. They were terrified and scattered in all directions, trampling grass and zinnias alike. But turkeys have a strong herd instinct and they soon came back to huddle together in the pen.

When it came time to market the birds, a little girl from a neighboring farm volunteered to drive them into town. She simply trailed along behind them with a long stick clutched in her hand and the turkeys would go down the road like a small tidal wave of white feathers. At the railroad station, the turkeys would obligingly cram themselves into a cage and that was all there was to it. The railroad took over after that, and in due time I would receive a check for my scant labors.

Since Sherwood's zinnias were blooming, he decided they needed no further attention and abandoned them entirely. He began driving about in his car to the nearby fields and farms, making friends and getting to know all about farming. The farmers, unlike the mountaineers, took to him at once, and he would come home with his car loaded up with an embarrassment of riches he had been unable to refuse — bottles of homemade wine, bushels of apples and fresh eggs. All our neighbors were terribly poor and I was afraid they might have gone hungry in order to show Sherwood that he was welcome and well liked. But, he said, they would seem so hurt if he turned down a gift, he was unable to do it.

I had a wonderful time riding about the country on

horseback. It was wild, untouched and untamed land and in some of the remote parts the people spoke almost Elizabethan English. On one hot day, I had been riding for some hours when I saw a young girl in a Mother Hubbard, digging potatoes. I reined up close to her and asked where I might find a spring to drink from. She stood up, squinted at me, and in the very low voice of the mountaineers said, "Yon way."

I was beginning to realize, with some surprise, that I shared some of Sherwood's feelings about being close to the earth. I loved living on the farm, despite the hard work and some disagreeable conditions.

Food was an ever pressing problem. Our meals were determined by what kind of food happened to be available, for we had an icebox but no ice. We learned to accept warm drinks as our neighbors did and we had a cellar in which to store food. It was not cold enough to keep milk longer than overnight, but we kept our eggs and chickens and wildfowl there.

Our supply of staples was a constant consideration, for it was a long trip to the mill to buy flour and almost as far to the store to buy other things. Neighboring farmers would come around and ask, "Would you like some pork? We just did the slaughtering," or, "Here's some lamb and beef, fresh killed."

We bought meat when it was so offered to us and this

determined the nature of our menus. We found out that smoked hams would keep indefinitely and that even slightly cooked pork would keep if it was buried in a jar of its own fat.

After some time, we had developed a good garden by carefully planning the planting of the vegetables so they would mature in a regulated succession. Sherwood found the asparagus I had planted one day and to him it looked tender and succulent. He pulled some up like carrots and proudly brought it in to show me. As tactfully as I could I explained the nature of asparagus; it has to remain buried until ripe.

Except for the gardening, the farm did not fare well. We had a cow that gave no milk and my horse was a determined and dedicated rover. It visited all the other farms to sample alien hay and someone was forever coming over to complain about the infernal horse. Finally I shut him up but he was clever and learned how to open the gate and escape.

One man was beside himself with indignation that my horse had helped itself to a full meal of his hay. He ranted and carried on and finally I said to Sherwood, "For heavens' sakes, this is just silly. We can't spend this much time quarreling over a horse. Why doesn't he just ask to be paid for his hay? And for that matter why doesn't he keep his gates shut?"

But the affair seemed to have been raised to the lofty heights of principle. The farmer was too angry to listen to reason and he stomped away, threatening to sue.

"Forget about it," I told Sherwood. "He can't possibly get more than the cost of the hay. Let it go. Let him win his ridiculous case."

But "his ridiculous case" came to trial. The court was held in an open field, in a small clearing at the foot of a hill. A lawyer had been asked to serve as arbiter and judge, and Sherwood and the still irate farmer faced him in the fresh air, under a pale blue, cloud-laced sky.

I sat on a nearby bank, unable to restrain myself from giggling. They were all being so deadly serious about the whole thing, which could have been a scene from a Gilbert and Sullivan operetta. First the farmer told his side of the rape of his haystack. He pounded his fist into his hand and glared at me angrily for laughing. Then the lawyer-judge allowed Sherwood to wax eloquent on such stirring subjects as freedom for horses and good fences make good neighbors. Finally the lawyer deliberated.

The case was decided in favor of the farmer and Sherwood meekly handed over five dollars. When it was all over, I was somewhat indignant about the decision of the court. "I think that's wrong," I told Sherwood as we drove home. "I think they should at least have admitted it was his fault as much as ours for leaving his gate open."

"I thought you said to let him off."

"Well, I didn't mean after the case was already being tried."

I did not mind the five dollars certainly but I had a feeling that the farmer had been out to take us because we were not natives. Most of the people, however, had begun to feel we belonged there and even the bootleggers had accepted us. Sherwood asked me one night if I cared to go along with him to call on a bootlegger that John Greear had told him about.

I agreed to go and late on that moonless night we set off. Sherwood drove for so long down so many winding roads that I was convinced we were lost. I decided not to say anything and simply sat there silently as he drove. He stopped from time to time, as if to get his bearings.

Finally Sherwood said, "Are you sure you really want to go? Maybe it's dangerous."

Then I was sure he was lost and wanted a way out of his predicament without admitting it. "Of course I want to go."

To my surprise, Sherwood promptly turned off the road onto a narrow lane that went up to a ramshackle old house set in a small, not very clear clearing among tall scraggly pines. Sherwood blinked his lights three times, waited a moment, then blinked them again. He got out of the car and I scrambled out after him, determined not to be left alone.

We picked our way cautiously through bottles and rotting pieces of wood to the back door of the house. We waited. I knew that unseen eyes were measuring us as we stood there.

After a long time, we heard shuffling noises inside and an arm snaked through the partly opened door, holding a jug. Sherwood took the jug, placed the proper sum of money in the extended hand, and we went back to the car and hastily drove away.

It was a custom of the country, or had once been, to have a jug of White Mule set out on the gatepost along with a tin cup. Anyone who happened along was supposed to have a drink and a sociable visit. We only tried that once, just to see if we would draw anybody amusing. As it happened, only Mrs. Greear came that day and she did not drink. She glanced at the jug with surprise and perhaps disapproval, and when she had gone away, we retired the jug to the cellar.

I was glad we had disposed of the jug a few days later when a kindly little old lady came to call on me. We chatted awhile and for some reason she was highly concerned about how we were getting along on the farm.

She was very poor herself, thin and obviously over-worked. She lived alone in an unpainted mountain cabin on a side road near our house and she had great dignity.

When we had talked for some time she said, "Well, you certainly don't strike me as uppity people, so I just thought I ought to warn you. I hear your husband writes books."

I allowed as how that was true.

She sighed. "We're very poor around here, you know, and a good many folks don't read nor write. You should tell your husband that nobody around here ever buys any books."

Another day, a thin blond girl came looking for work. She was so shy that it was hard to get her to talk, but finally she told me her story. She was about sixteen and had been married for a number of years already. That was the custom of the country. All the girls got married the instant they were able to, and it did not matter to whom. This poor girl had been unlucky enough to marry a bootlegger. A week earlier, someone had informed on him and he had completely vanished. His friends had smuggled him out of the country at night, for no one was on the side of the Federal men, the hated revenuers.

Now the girl was alone and I hired her to wash dishes and clean the house. I would have been better off doing everything myself, for the girl was a pale wraith who would sit down in whatever room I was in and silently stare at me for hours. It made me uneasy to have a mute, dispassionate audience for my every move, but that was the way with the local people. They felt no compulsion to fill holes in the air with idle talk.

We would often have callers, neighbors who would troop in with all their children to "pay their respects." They would arrange themselves around the front room and settle down sociably. Then there would be absolute silence unless I could think of something to say. At first I was desperate, then I learned that they did not mind long-drawn-out silences. On one such call, one of the younger daughters clutched a small posy of violets in her fist for at least forty-five minutes, while the rest of the family sat around stiffly. Then the mother said, "Give it to her, Gertrude Betty." The girl jerked herself upright and handed me the flowers. After another half hour, they all stood as if on signal, nodded and departed, having done their neighborly duty.

For months, Sherwood had been exploring the land around the house, marveling at the stones and rocks and vowing to build something with them one day. Then we heard from Horace Liveright that *Dark Laughter* was still doing very well and was, indeed, a best seller. Sherwood decided to go ahead with his house.

Bill Spratling was still teaching architecture at Tulane and he sent up a set of plans he had designed for the new house, but Sherwood did not know how to read them. Neither did Mr. Ball, the builder Sherwood had hired. But Mr. Ball was confident he could build the house that Sherwood described to him in glowing terms.

Mr. Ball was a tall mountain man with a commanding nose and a square, heavy jaw. He looked exactly like the Gilbert Stuart portraits of George Washington, with the same ill-fitting teeth bulging out the mouth just enough to make him look somewhat disapproving. He appeared to have just about forgotten how to read and write. As the work on the house began, he would jot down a few figures on a loose shingle, and that was the extent of his calculations. He was around seventy years old and told us he had been famous as a moonshiner when he was younger. He could curse for ten minutes at a time without once uttering a single curse I had heard before. If one of his young workers did something to displease him, he would begin, "You young scallawaggle . . ." and go on from there, with rich, rolling invention.

Mr. Ball hired farmers from nearby farms, even though there was no one who had ever tried to build a stone house before. They hauled stones out of Ripshin Creek and from hillsides and pastures and the mountain-

145

eers brought stones down out of the mountains and the hollows. It seemed that every stone for miles around would be used in the house, but there were always more. Great beams of seasoned oak were cut and stacked in readiness.

The stone walls were painstakingly laid, eighteen inches thick. Mr. Ball scrambled around the beams and rafters with such monkey-like agility it was hard to believe he was the same grave, gray man he seemed on the ground. Sherwood was everywhere, directing and suggesting and often simply in the way. He was completely caught up in the house building project, as if it were his greatest novel and demanded total involvement.

Everything came to a dead halt. Mr. Ball told Sherwood he had laid the men off for a few days. Sherwood asked him why but Mr. Ball would not explain. He just insisted that it was necessary. Only later did we find out what had happened.

Mr. Ball was a proud man and needed to give expression to his pride. He had hired a man to drive him around in a car. He loaded several jugs of White Mule into the back of the car and relaxed, sipping and sampling, while the driver took him around to one farmhouse after another. At each, he would park the car, offer the farmer a drink and brag, "I'm going to build a house that will last until Gabriel blows his horn." When he grew tired, the driver parked the car in the shade and Mr. Ball would sleep until he felt the urge to have another drink.

Three days later, Mr. Ball was back on the job, completely refreshed and ready to throw himself into the monumental task of building the house. He remarked only that it relaxed him to go on a bender every once in a while.

When Mr. Ball saw the orchard on our property he told me the apples were called "Farmers' Friends." I asked him why. "Well," he said, squinting in the way that he did when he was about to make an amusing remark, "you can keep 'em in the cellar for years and years and they ain't worth a damn when you do eat 'em."

One day an old man came around and told Sherwood and Mr. Ball he was a stonecutter. He was a large man and had once been powerful, but he was bent nearly double because he was dying of stomach cancer.

Sherwood pitied the old man but doubted that he knew anything about stone cutting, for few men in that region did. "Do you think he really is?" he asked Mr. Ball.

Mr. Ball scratched his head and said, "I've walked these roads, man and boy, for thirty years and some of the best men I knowed is liars."

Sherwood and Mr. Ball told the old man he could cut the arch for the fireplace and they would pay him five

147

dollars, but only if he finished the job. The old man went to the fireplace and started measuring, tying and retying knots in a dirty old piece of string. He kept mumbling to himself that he would show them all what kind of stonecutter he was. None of us expected him to be able to do it. It was a complicated piece of work that even Mr. Ball was not sure how to handle.

Then the old man climbed into his ancient wagon and drove off and we were sure it was the last we would ever hear of him. In a few weeks we got the news that the old man had died. Mr. Ball had a coffin built for him and went to the old man's funeral. When Mr. Ball came to work the next day, he approached Sherwood.

"I got a hunch," he said. "Let's go take a look-see where that old man lived. No telling but what he might have cut that stone."

They drove up the side of a mountain on a winding road to the old man's cabin and looked around. They found the stones in a shed behind the cabin, carefully arranged on the dirt floor. They loaded them into the car and drove back to fit them around the fireplace. It formed a perfect arch. The old man must have spent the last of his strength in painfully chiseling away at the stone until he had completed the job he had set out to do.

The old man had, indeed, shown them all what kind of stonecutter he was. I felt as though the fireplace arch would be his monument, the one no one could afford to place over his grave.

Before the house was done there was yet another stone arch to be cut, and this time no stonecutter came down from the hills to volunteer for the job. Instead, people from all around began to bring in stones that might fit, jigsaw fashion, into the arch. They laid out the stones on the ground in the form of an arch and looked everywhere for stones that would work into the pattern. Sherwood wandered for days, searching for exactly the right size and shape of stone. At last the pattern was completed, and Mr. Ball asked one of the men to fit it all into place.

Sherwood and I and several of the workers stood around watching the man work at assembling the arch. He did a fine job of it, and when the show was over everyone went off for lunch.

When Sherwood returned to take another look at the arch, he flew into a fury. During the lunch hour the worker had proudly chiseled his name in large, awkward letters, square in the center of the arch. Sherwood directed a fiery stream of invective at the man until he ran out of breath. When he stopped, the workman picked up his lunch pail and started walking down the road. Sherwood went after him and I could see that he was ashamed of some of the things he had said. I watched

149

them talking and then Sherwood came back and told me of the exchange.

"He quit. Said I shouldn't have talked to him like that in front of all the others."

"What about those terrible letters on the rock?" I asked. "Will we have to take them all down again?"

Sherwood shook his head. "No, he's coming back on Sunday when there's nobody here to chisel off the lettering."

"Well that's good anyway," I said, then stopped. Sherwood was looking at me quizzically.

"Know what else he said? He asked me if I write books and I said yes. Then he asked me if I put my name on my books." Sherwood paused a moment, then added, "There wasn't a damn thing I could say to that."

Our last crisis was in the plastering of the walls. When all the rooms but one had been finished, the men decided to start the celebration for the completion of the house while plastering the final room.

Sherwood and I heard the wild, gleeful cries coming from the house and decided we would investigate before the house could be torn down, stone by stone, as it had been put up. The sounds of revelry made me decide to stay outside while Sherwood went to find out what was happening.

He soon returned, with a gob of white plaster on his shoulder. In the final room to be plastered, he told me, the plaster was a gooey foot deep on the floor and an inch thick on all the men. Only one of the workmen was a professional plasterer, but all the men were tipsily eager to have a go at it. They were clambering up the scaffold in turns, slamming great trough-loads of sloppy plaster at the ceiling before teetering down again. Half the men were wallowing in the stuff on the floor. Only the huge jug of moonshine was intact, though emptied. "They threw plaster at me," Sherwood said rather plaintively. "Said I should have a try at it."

We stared at each other in silence for a moment, then turned and walked back to the farmhouse without a word. The next day, the men came back and cleaned up the mess and the professional plasterer redid the walls and the ceiling.

It was August in 1926 and the house called Ripshin was finished. Sherwood had good reason to be proud of it. He had taken joy in every phase of its construction and it had an unusual, unorthodox beauty. The main living room was thirty feet long. The master bedroom had a great stone fireplace, with the massive stone arch, mute memorial to the dead craftsman. Outside, there was a fine terrace of stone. It all seemed to have naturally risen from the rocky countryside, completely one with the surroundings. It was a thoroughly masculine house, with heavy furniture and straightforward simplicity.

But Sherwood could find joy only in the building of the house, not in contemplation of the finished product, just as he could find no satisfaction in the mere fact of his earlier books. While building Ripshin, he had felt only mildly guilty about the weekly check that kept coming from Horace Liveright. Now the house was finished and he had no reason not to set up a regular schedule of writing, but he found that he could not. Whether he felt that he had written about all the things that were in him to write about, or whether he simply felt his writing days were over, he was unable to write anything that had any sense or meaning for him. He grew steadily more morose during that fall until, in December, he decided he needed a change of pace and scene.

With forced jauntiness, he suggested a trip to Paris. He may have secretly believed that seeing his old friends in France would somehow renew his wellspring of creativity, but no matter what the motive, I welcomed the idea. Perhaps Sherwood had been out of touch with writers too long. In Troutdale, people had accepted him as a friendly neighbor, without a thought to his writing. Sherwood might need some reassurance of his reputation as a literary figure, and certainly Paris would provide him with that. If anything, he was more highly regarded there than in his own country.

We made plans, each our own, and it was not until we reached New York that I discovered what Sherwood's plans included.

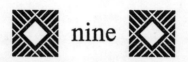 nine

It was December of 1926 and the New Yorkers we saw on the streets were bustling about with the glazed-eye look that is peculiar to shoppers. While we waited in our hotel for the sailing date of the ship, Sherwood calmly announced that he had invited his two younger children, John and Mimi, to come along with us, as a sort of Christmas present for them.

I controlled a quick flare of anger at not having been informed of this earlier. I simply asked him how he had managed that.

"Oh, I just wrote to Cornelia and she said it would be all right. They should be getting into New York any day now."

After some soul-searching, his as well as mine, I decided not to be upset about it. Being angry with Sherwood's impulsiveness was like being angry with the color of his eyes. If the two young children could get along with a stepmother they had never met before, the stepmother would be able to cope with them.

John and Mimi did not reach New York until almost the sailing day and it was only on the boat that I met them for the first time. Mimi was a sweet little girl of sixteen, with long black hair and a round face like her mother's. John was three years older and seemed gentler and more sensitive than Sherwood's other boy, Robert. I liked both children from the start but I was unfortunately not able to show this to them for several days. The seasickness I had pointlessly anticipated on Lake Pontchartrain caught up with me now and I spent the first three days at sea down below in my cabin.

When I was able to move around again, John and Mimi had made friends with just about everybody on the boat. Sherwood's natural facility for getting to know people had been passed along to them. While I had been ill, the steward had asked Mimi how her mother liked her tea, and she had gravely replied, "I am sure I do not know."

I spent the rest of the voyage getting to know the children and making friends with them. Sherwood, of course, had become fascinated with the mechanics of running a ship and passed most of the time with the crew members, exploring the holds and the engine rooms.

One day Mimi decided she no longer liked the length of her hair. She had spent all her life in a small town in Illinois and had been very much impressed with the chic, stylishly turned out women she had seen in New York and on the boat. On impulse, she chopped off her hair at what she thought to be the fashionable level.

Her hair now hung to her ears, perfectly straight and perfectly terrible. John was shocked. He had been scrupulous about looking after his little sister, but there was nothing he could have done to foresee this. At first Mimi was quite pleased with herself, but then she must have seen the outcome mirrored in our eyes, for she sank into a slow panic.

I was relieved to find that there was a hairdresser on board and I quickly hustled Mimi off to have a repair job done before Sherwood could see what had happened to his daughter. The hairdresser scissored and shaped, curled and combed, and the end result was attractive. Sherwood liked the new hair style and looked rather speculatively, I thought, at my own long hair but made no suggestions about it.

In Paris, John went to live with a French family so he could learn the language and the customs of the country. I found a French school for Mimi and went shopping with her to buy suitable clothes. Those she had were fine for a small Midwest town, but not pert enough for Paris. After that, whenever she had time off from school, she would come to see me and go wandering through the fashionable shops, gradually learning what high style was all about.

The children had proven to be much less of a problem that I had originally expected. They stayed on in Paris even after Sherwood and I returned and finally came back with my sister Dorothea and her husband, Max Radin.

The hotel that Sherwood and I found to stay in was on the Left Bank. It was old and cheap but it had the advantage of being open all through the night so that we could get in at any hour. Most hotels of that type in Paris have razor-eyed concierges who guard their domains like trolls.

It was January in Paris and the air was crisp and clean, reminding me of Michigan winters without snow. It carried, at times, the burnt smell of chestnuts roasting on open braziers and the marvelous smell of freshly baked French bread from the many little bakeries dotted around. Overhead, the trees formed bleak latticeworks of barren branches that scraped and rustled in the cold wind.

Sherwood wanted to be left alone in the mornings so that he could write, and I found a girl who made a living by guiding Americans around to the various sights. She took me all over Paris, showing me the older and most interesting parts of the city. I enjoyed the outings, but when I went back to the hotel, Sherwood would be in a surly mood, for he was not finding it any easier to write.

Sherwood wrote to Paul Rosenfeld, a literary critic and a close friend, that he felt as if he were in a rowboat in the middle of an ocean. He would row in one direction for a while, then, finding nothing there, he would turn and row in another direction for a time. Sherwood drew his depression around him like a shell and would emerge only on rare occasions. Very often he would be unable to shake off his black mood, even when he was with other people. But from time to time he would relax enough to see his old friends in Paris.

We went often to visit Gertrude Stein and Alice B. Toklas at her now-famous home at 27 rue de Fleurus. There would always be a cheerful fire burning in the large fireplace and the room was warm and comfortable. We were served small delicious cakes that Miss Toklas had baked, and mirabelle or framboise liqueurs in small carved glasses.

I had been warned that Gertrude Stein wanted only to talk to the husbands while Alice B. Toklas took charge of entertaining the wives, and when we first went to visit, I was quite intimidated. The walls of the house were covered with paintings that any museum would envy. There were paintings and drawings by Picasso, Gris, Matisse, Cézanne and dozens of other famous or future-famous artists.

I soon learned that the warning had been exaggerated, for both women did all they could to make me feel comfortable. The conversation was easy and relaxed. Both Sherwood and Gertrude had a profound interest in the Civil War and would spend hours talking about it. Both agreed that Lee had been highly overrated and that Grant was the central figure of the war. Gertrude had a firm conviction that even Lincoln was a lesser personage than Grant, but Sherwood could not go along with that. Nevertheless, they even discussed collaborating on a book about Grant.

I was not greatly interested in the Civil War at that time and I talked mostly with Alice Toklas, who was a quiet and retiring woman. We got along famously, having a mutual bond in our enjoyment of cooking. She was a superb cook and told me a great many things about fine cuisine. I was able to tell her about certain American dishes she had forgotten.

The two women were entirely unlike in their appearance and disposition. Gertrude was a massively built woman with long dark hair arranged in a simple bun like those the frontierswomen once wore for sheer practicality. Her nose was large and commanding and her eyes were set deep in her head and marvelously alive. She had an almost sculptured quality to her that Jo Davidson had caught perfectly in his 1923 statue of her. Alice was a rather thin, gypsy-like creature with dark short hair that was arranged to look like that of the sphinx. Her face had a calm, imperturbable quality that was reflected in her eyes. Alice maintained a genteel reserved air, while Gertrude was more robust, more inclined to bursts of easy laughter and voluble conversation.

One day, when we dropped in at 27 rue de Fleurus, Alice was just in the process of cutting Gertrude's hair. She told us that she had been working at it for some time already and I privately thought she had gone a good deal too far. It was only about an inch long now and Alice was still snipping away. Gertrude asked Sherwood how he liked it.

He stared at her new image for a long time and finally said, "Well, it makes you look like a monk."

I was shocked, certain that he had offended her, and I was about to apologize for him when I was stopped by Gertrude's laughter. She was highly pleased with the observation and perhaps she had intended exactly that effect.

We often met Ralph Church at Gertrude Stein's house. He was working for his doctorate at Oxford University and had been my brother's favorite student. He was a handsome, lively boy and completely irrepressible.

Gertrude invited Sherwood and me and Ralph Church to attend a poetry reading session at the salon of Miss Natalie Barney, a rich American woman who was a dogmatic patroness of the arts. Miss Barney's house was not far from our hotel and we all walked over to it. It was a fine old-fashioned place with red velvet plush chairs and heavy draperies that were bordered in gold braid. Everything was oversized and expensive and very antique. There was a small garden in which there sat, to our astonishment and glee, a small Greek temple of love.

Here, people sat in rows of rickety chairs, facing the temple and awaiting the poetry reading. I sat with Ralph in one row and Sherwood sat with Gertrude and Alice in the row ahead. A tall, emaciated English lady with burning eyes stood up and droned out her poetry, which had to do with some mystical, complicated concept of love.

161

Next to me, I could feel Ralph shake with suppressed laughter, and suddenly the absurdity of what we were doing and listening to struck me too. I began to shake with the same held-in mirth. Neither of us dared to laugh aloud, but we were almost sick from holding it back, making odd, snuffling noises as we tried. Sherwood shot me an admonishing glance, but I could see the quivering of his shoulders when the gaunt giantess began chanting some impossible lyric about the Isle of Lesbos. Mercifully it was brief, and we contained ourselves until we were outside and some distance down the street. Then we collapsed into great shouts of near hysterical, helpless laughter.

Some time later, Gertrude decided to hold a party in Sherwood's honor because many of her friends wanted to meet him. Sherwood thanked her for the gesture and I thought no more about it until I was dressing to go to the party. When I was ready to go, Sherwood was still lounging dispiritedly in an easy chair.

"Why don't you get dressed?" I asked.

"I can't go," he said, without moving. "I've got the flu."

"Sherwood, that's nonsense. You get up and get dressed. You're invited to meet all these people who are coming and you're the only reason she's holding the party at all."

"I'm too sick. You go over without me."

I argued with him for a while longer but he was adamant. The only illness he had was his depression but he insisted he had the flu. Finally I went to the party alone and terribly embarrassed. I could hardly tell Gertrude and Alice that Sherwood was sulking or say: "My husband is an idiot."

Alice Toklas was very sweet about it. She fixed it up with everybody by telling them that Sherwood was sick and could not come. There were a lot of Americans at the party who had no reason to be there except to meet Sherwood and no reason to stay if he was not present. They drifted away gradually, but I stayed behind in order to apologize to Gertrude and try to explain the situation to her.

Gertrude said: "My dear, you don't have to explain to me. I know exactly what happened."

They were both very sympathetic and insisted that I stay on for a while. A painter dropped in, and then a writer and, as it turned out, the second, unplanned party was very pleasant indeed.

When I got home, Sherwood was sitting in the same chair drinking whiskey and apparently having a good time all by himself, as if he had been able to exorcise his gloom by giving in to it.

One name that was rarely mentioned in Gertrude

Stein's house was James Joyce. Sherwood had met him through Sylvia Beach, the owner of the famous bookstore Shakespeare and Company. It seemed to me that Gertrude considered Joyce to be a rival literary luminary and did not want to talk about him. Indeed, she had only met him once, briefly.

James Joyce was a thin man, somewhat stooped and oddly graceful. His manner was so distinguished that one tended not to notice the slight shabbiness of his clothes. His eyes were dark blue and so weak that he habitually wore dark, thick glasses.

Some time after Sherwood had met him, Joyce sent a note to our hotel, inviting us both to dinner. At the appointed time, he came to the hotel to pick us up, but Sherwood had decided to have a relapse of his "flu" and refused to go out. What was worse, he insisted that I go to dinner with Joyce in a way that I could not refuse in front of the man. I was even more embarrassed than I had been at Gertrude's party, for of course the poor man had no interest in taking me to dinner. It was Sherwood he wanted to talk to.

James Joyce took me to the Tour d'Argent, which was a fine and very expensive restaurant. I looked over the menu and found something that was not too costly and then I asked Mr. Joyce what he was going to have. He looked rather uneasy as he told me, "Milk." He added that he had indigestion, but it did not make me feel much better. I forced myself to finish all of the dinner, well aware that he had long since finished his glass of warmed milk.

I ate, trying not to bolt the food down but also trying to finish the meal with reasonable dispatch. Joyce informed me that a dog had bitten him when he was only five years old and that he had been terrified of dogs ever since. He stroked the thin goatee he wore and remarked that he had grown it to conceal the scar from the dog bite.

That was the extent of our conversation. I had not read his books and had no intention of ever trying to read *Ulysses*. It seemed to me that Joyce wanted his readers to learn a special language to read his book and I was unwilling to do so. I remarked on this to Sherwood and he said simply, "If you don't understand it, don't read it."

After Joyce's brief commentary on dogs, we sat in stiff, guarded silence, neither of us relaxed enough to talk. Then he politely escorted me back to the hotel and left me alone with my anger at Sherwood for having subjected me to the ordeal.

Because of this kind of incident, Ralph Church got the impression that I was unhappy with Sherwood. When he returned to the United States he told my brother that

Sherwood was unkind to me, which upset my family considerably.

Sherwood was not being ugly only to me, but to everybody around him, and most particularly to himself. The only reason that I was unhappy was that Sherwood was so miserable. He simply could not write and it destroyed his peace of mind.

I continued to leave him alone in the mornings, knowing he wanted no one to watch him agonize over unfilled pages. I knew a number of people, but often I was forced to attend dull little tea parties at which the women sat around telling each other about special addresses where special goods and services could be found. I was bored with the proceedings and when anyone asked me, as they inevitably came around to doing, "And what do you do?" I would tell them, "I raise pigs."

On one such afternoon, I met a large and jolly man named Berg who had come to Paris with a redheaded woman, not his wife. She had, however, used his wife's passport, and when his actual wife wanted to join him there was trouble. The officials told her: "You can't go to Paris; you're already there." That day I was wearing a lovely new dress I had just bought, white satin trimmed with crystal beads. I was sitting near the window, listening to the comic problems of the Bergs, when a large cat came in from the roof and leaped onto my lap. I have a great weakness for cats and I allowed it to sit on my lap for a long time. When it was finally time to go, I stood up and there was a huge cat-shaped black mark on my white satin dress.

It did not bother me a whit, but when Sherwood saw it he was horrified. "You can't afford to be so casual about your clothes," he told me. "You know you can't afford dresses like that."

I had been bored that day to the point of insouciance. "What do you care?" I asked. "You didn't pay for it."

That annoyed him too, for it was a point of difference, if not actual contention, between us. I did not have a great deal of money of my own, but enough to be occasionally independent. I suspect it bothered Sherwood that I was not more completely dependent on him.

Together, Sherwood and I often went to Sylvia Beach's Shakespeare and Company at 12 rue de l'Odéon. Sylvia was a small and lively woman who was delightful. It was she who had first introduced Gertrude Stein to Sherwood on his first visit to Paris and she had helped him in many other ways. Her bookshop was small and crowded with the best of American books. The walls were covered over and overlapping with photographs of artists and writers she knew. I was naturally interested in comparing her bookshop experiences with my own at the Doubleday Doran store. I found that there were almost no similarities.

Sylvia told me that it was easier to lend books in France than to sell them because of the rigid frugality of the French and the bohemian poverty of the Americans on the Left Bank. Sylvia ran her lending library on what the French called *le plan américain,* though I saw nothing that smacked of American superefficiency. She kept no card titles and no catalogue. Instead, if someone wanted a book, he could either browse about until he found it, or ask Sylvia where it was. She did have a loosely kept file of members' cards, each with the name and last known address of the member, the date of subscription, the deposit, and the names of the books taken out. Any member was able to take books for as long as he pleased. Sylvia told me that Joyce took out dozens of books and kept them for years.

Her membership file read like a roll call of American and French writers, including such figures as André Gide, André Malraux, James Joyce, Ezra Pound, Scott Fitzgerald, Ernest Hemingway, and dozens of others. Gertrude Stein had been a member, but when Sylvia published Joyce's *Ulysses,* she and Alice went to the bookshop to announce that they had transferred their account to the American Library on the Right Bank.

Gertrude had an old, odd enmity for Joyce, as there was room for only one experimentalist in Paris, in her view.

Adrienne Monnier had a French bookshop at 7 rue de l'Odéon, just across the street from Shakespeare and Company, and she and Sylvia were great friends. Adrienne invited Sherwood and me to dinner and prepared a magnificent *poule* in the French way. Adrienne talked to Sherwood in pidgin English and he responded in pidgin French, but somehow they understood each other and got along famously. She introduced us to her sister, who made very unusual embroidery pictures, much like tapestry. Later, Sherwood tried to place some of her work with New York art dealers, but never had much success with it.

Hemingway was in Paris at that time, but we saw little of him, not by our design, but perhaps by his. Sherwood appeared to have forgotten all about *The Torrents of Spring*, but I had not, quite. Sherwood thought the book had been simply foolish; I thought it both foolish and vindictive.

I was visiting with Gertrude and Alice without Sherwood one day when Hemingway bounced into the room, beating his chest and loudly boasting: "I can walk like an Olympic marathoner. I just walked all the way over here — fifteen blocks — and I'm not a bit tired."

Only minutes before, I had walked twenty blocks to

Gertrude's house and I had not been a bit tired either, so his heroic feat failed to impress me. Hemingway regularly let everyone know about his superior prowess at skiing or boxing or some other manly sport. The skiers I knew in Paris told me he was really quite poor at it.

Hemingway came to see us at our hotel and spent some time making fun of the hotel and how shabby and poorly run the place was.

"Keep in mind that they're very nice to us here," I snapped at him. "That's why we came here and that's why we're staying here."

When Hemingway left, Sherwood told me I had been rude to poor Ernest. It was true; I had been. I had meant to be.

Gertrude once told Hemingway, "After all, you are ninety per cent Rotarian."

"Can't you make it eighty per cent?" he asked, trying to make it a joke.

"No," she said, with sincere regret, "I can't."

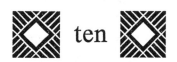 ten

It was the end of our time in Paris, for Sherwood had
developed a curious nostalgia for Virginia and the
earthy, folksy people we knew there. We were talking
about it when, as if to present a sharp and startling contrast to those people, two young artists came to see us.
They were having a show just up the street from the
École des Beaux-Arts, and were having trouble with
government officials who thought it was disgusting to
have such immoral paintings in the store window.

We walked over to view the controversial window
for ourselves, and I had to privately admit that the government had a point. One of the artists had stationed
himself in a chair at the doorway and was ostentatiously

171

cradling a pistol in his lap. He informed me that he was defending modern art and that the paintings in the window were every bit as good as Picasso and that the whole world would one day know it.

We wished him good luck and strolled on down the street toward Robert Duncan's house. Robert was Isadora's brother and affected a long, flowing beard, Greek robes and sandals. We peered through the open doorway for a moment, nonplussed, watching Robert vacuum-cleaning his garden patio, taking tender care with the vacuum hose on his plants. Then we walked on, our thoughts entirely focused on our country neighbors near Ripshin.

Ripshin had not changed at all in our absence. It still stood with stony pride and the brook it had been named for still cut its gleaming course through the winter-wasted fields. Our two dogs, Rip and Shin, did not recognize me. They simply looked at me without interest, then turned and trotted off toward the barn. Suddenly it seemed to occur to both of them at once. Together they turned, took another look, and raced toward me, yelping and whining with joy. I was overcome, both by the onslaught of dogs and the sudden emotion of being home.

Sherwood went off on a lecture tour, partly to pay for

some of the construction costs of Ripshin, but partly because of his compelling need to wander, a need that was never to desert him in his life. I busied myself with home and garden and rode for hours each day, upsetting many good country folk who thought it improper for a woman to wear jodhpurs and to ride astraddle.

The same pale, faded blond girl came to wash dishes and to sit for long hours in the living room. One day I was searching for a small Italian silver box with a blue turquoise cover, set with stones. Stark Young had brought it back from Europe for me. It was gone. "Oh dear," I thought. "We've got a servant who steals."

I did not say anything about it, but I feel sure that my attitude toward the poor girl must have perceptibly altered. Finally Sherwood came back from his tour and gave me the silver box, now hopelessly broken.

"I'm sorry I broke your little box," he said. "I can have it fixed at the jewelers."

For a moment I was furious that he had taken it without telling me, then I realized that he had just taken a fancy to it and wanted something nice to look at while he was away from his home. If I had known he had taken it, I would not have expected to see it again. He lost things, or broke them, or they simply disappeared. It did not matter to him that the box was mine. Anything that he wanted was his in his own house.

173

His son Bob was going back after a vacation from the University of Virginia and the weather was cool. Sherwood told him, "Here's something you ought to have."

He picked up a very expensive and finely woven woolen blanket I had just bought. I did not think that Sherwood had even noticed it before, though I had placed it in a prominent spot in the house, but now he casually presented it to Bob.

If anything, Sherwood was in a worse mood than in Paris. Now he seemed to transfer to me his own self-irritation at not being able to write. He seemed to believe that it was I who was keeping him from writing. I was devoted to him, and unhappy because he was unhappy, but I did not know what I could do to help him.

At first I thought it was the same kind of depression that he had suffered so many times before, but then he began to be subtly cruel and hard.

There was a young man who operated a free-wheeling casual business of taking people for airplane rides around the country. He charged two dollars for the then novel and thrilling treat. Sherwood said to me, "Let's go and look the thing over. If the plane looks safe, we'll go up."

We did, and though the plane did not look at all safe by my own 1927 standards, Sherwood got into the plane and was flown off for a tour that lasted about twenty minutes. The rickety plane held only one passenger and I thought Sherwood was being gallant in testing the plane before I ventured into it.

But when he landed, he said to me, "You want to try it?" in a voice that clearly implied that he had seen it all and that it was time to go home.

I pretended not to notice his tone of voice and said that I certainly would like to try it. I was flown around for the same tour, but I was so irritated by Sherwood's surly behavior, I hardly noticed I was flying. When we landed, Sherwood was waiting for me in the car, staring grimly ahead. He refused to look at me or to say a word all the way back to the house.

That was the beginning of a new phase of my life with Sherwood, and it took me some time to realize that for reasons unknown to me, I annoyed him terribly. I had no idea if I had changed or he had, but I kept thinking that the mood would go away. It did not.

After a few weeks, I began to think that I should go to New York, simply to get away and allow him to live peacefully. I suggested it, but he said, "That's not for you. Don't go to New York."

In Paris, Sherwood sometimes managed to break through his depression and laugh and talk, and everyone would be so happy to see the old Sherwood again.

Now he never smiled and the oppressive atmosphere in the house was haunting.

Then there came a time when Sherwood and I would take long, terrible drives through the country, neither of us saying a word for hours, cloaked in bitter, choking silence. I tried to get out of going along with him at times, but he insisted that I come along for a reason that became shatteringly clear to me.

We were driving along a deserted road, nearly in North Carolina. The road had a soft shoulder that fell away to a deep slope. Without any preamble, Sherwood said, in a strange blank voice, "I wish it were all over." With that, he twisted the wheel and we went over the edge.

We skittered and slid and nearly toppled over, but somehow the car remained upright until the slope flattened out and then the car simply rolled to a halt in the middle of a field.

It was a grim illumination for me. I had not dreamed he was desperate enough to try to kill us both.

We sat in the car without talking for a long time. Finally it became clear to both of us that neither of us was going to broach the subject first. Then Sherwood set to work at the problem of getting the car back onto the road, while I stood in the field, feeling drained and empty.

Finally the car was headed back toward Ripshin. We returned without saying a word about the incident and never spoke of it after that.

For some time, Sherwood seemed to be in a better frame of mind, perhaps because he had purged from his mind the idea of death. That may have been when he devised the phrase he later asked to be etched on his tombstone: "Life, not death, is the great adventure."

At the end of August, Sherwood learned about the Smyth County Fair that was being held in Marion, a town of about four thousand people, a few miles from Ripshin. There were trotting races, which we both loved, so we went off to see the county fair and sat in the grandstand, watching the high-stepping fancy horses stir up flowers of dust on the track.

In the grandstand, Sherwood met a man named Denny Culbert and they began talking about the two local newspapers, the *Smyth County News* and the *Marion Democrat*, because both newspapers were for sale. Culbert suggested that Sherwood, because he was a writer, should buy the papers.

Almost at once the idea caught hold of Sherwood's fancy; his excitement grew visibly. He talked for a while longer with Culbert, but his interest was entirely on the notion of becoming a country editor. Within minutes we had left the grandstand without even a backward glance at the trotters. As we walked along Main Street, which was part of Highway Eleven, I looked around at the town. It was even smaller than Saginaw, where I was born. The building which housed both newspapers was just off Main Street, facing the county courthouse and surrounded by the Baptist, Lutheran and Presbyterian churches.

Sherwood was not a man to linger at the edges of an issue. When he had decided that the world of business was not for him, he walked out of his office for good. Now that he had made up his mind to own two newspapers, he strode directly into the office of Arthur L. Cox, who owned both papers.

Arthur Cox told him about the setup. The *Smyth County News* was Republican and the *Marion Democrat* was obviously Democratic. Since Cox himself was a Republican, he favored the *Smyth County News* and it consisted of eight pages while the *Marion Democrat* had only four. He admitted that he generally tried to steer advertising and new subscriptions to the *Smyth County News*. He added that he was asking twenty-five hundred dollars for each of the papers and that they would not be sold separately.

There was no doubt in Sherwood's mind. This was his destiny. On the spot, he told Cox that he would buy the papers and then he set about raising the money to pay for them.

Sherwood went off to New York to see Burton Emmett, who headed a large advertising agency and who had an absolute mania for collecting any scrap of paper that Sherwood had scribbled on. Some time earlier he had asked to be permitted to buy Sherwood's manuscripts, but Sherwood had never been able to figure out why on earth anyone would want them, so he had done nothing about the request. Now he needed the money.

Burton Emmett immediately agreed to lend Sherwood five thousand dollars without interest and Sherwood agreed to turn over his published and unpublished manuscripts and to try to convince other authors to sell their manuscripts to Emmett. He also agreed to repay the loan in about five years.

When he returned to Ripshin he was elated. I asked him how he intended to repay Burton Emmett, for it seemed that the newspapers would barely provide us with a living.

"He'll never miss it," Sherwood said airily, and added, "I told Horace that the deal's off."

While in New York, Sherwood had gone to Horace Liveright and told him not to send the hundred-dollar check any longer, because he felt oppressed by the pressing responsibility of writing a book a year. Now he would make his own living and write when he wanted to, or when he could. Horace had been astounded, Sherwood told me rather smugly. It had never entered his mind that a writer might refuse money.

We were definitely in the newspaper business, and within a month Sherwood was turning out his first issue. His initial move was to make both papers eight pages long and to confine political news to a single editorial column. He asked the sheriff to write the Democratic news for the *Marion Democrat* and the postmaster to write for the *Smyth County News*. That took care of politics as far as Sherwood was concerned. Then he raised the subscription rates from $1.25 to $1.75 a year, because he thought people would respect the papers more if they cost more.

Sherwood decided that his weekly newspapers would have nothing to do with state and national news, nor would they print the mass-produced "fillers," such as recipes for onion omelettes and stock market statistics. He would concentrate on the day-to-day news of the county, such as, "Who gets hurt during the fall threshing or shoots some fellow for getting gay with his wife," as he wrote in one of the first subscription blanks. Other country newspapers might print "ready-made" articles and fiction, but Sherwood printed such oddments as the Book of Ruth, a poem by Maxwell Bodenheim, Chateaubriand on the appreciation of cats, and several of his own short stories. Sometimes these "features" would fill an entire page with very fine print and I often wondered who in Smyth County was reading them.

Sherwood moved nearly a thousand books into the printshop and operated an informal lending library. He was especially delighted when the wife of a local workingman began reading Dostoyevsky. He enjoyed watching the faces of the people who came in when they saw the colored prints of Cézanne or Van Gogh he had hung on the wall. They would stare for an instant, scratch their heads and look away, pointedly making no comment.

There was a big stove in the room, and after a time the office was a social center, just as my father's drugstore had once been. People would drop in to pass along the news or to hear some and Sherwood was at the hub of it all. It seemed a perfect existence for him. All his life, Sherwood had harbored a longing for an intimate communion with small town life, which he considered the mainstream of America. It was a romantic notion and it is sadly rare that romanticism finds such perfect expression.

Sherwood's new role as Country Editor was enormous fun for him. We moved into a small apartment over the printshop and Sherwood made himself a part of the everyday life of the town. He went to all the court trials, rode around with the sheriff, went to sheep shearings and auctions and came to know all about all the people. It was fascinating for me to see the happenings about town be transformed in Sherwood's mind and be printed as his own deeply personal view of what had happened. Quite often it was widely separated from the mere facts. He cared nothing about "journalese" or the tradition of telling "who, what, where, and when" in the first paragraph. His articles were constructed along the lines of his short stories, with an initial "hook" to interest readers and a gradual buildup to a dramatic impact. He freely indulged his fancies and the *Roanoke Times* picked up a story he had written about an attempted holdup. The *Times* congratulated Sherwood for his "scoop." But as it turned out, the man who was supposed to have been held up denied the story and Sherwood wrote an amusing retraction of the story, bemoaning his betrayal by the informant. It was his only "scoop" and it had failed.

Sherwood cared little about the looks of his papers. There were few photographs because they were too expensive to print. Very rarely were there any headlines, for Sherwood maintained that one piece of news was just about as interesting as any other. He usually printed the same masthead, with scant regard for dates. Some of the heads were occasionally printed upside down and the numbering of pages was haphazard at best. The spelling was individual enough to make it appear almost as though the paper had been printed in dialect.

To Sherwood, these were trifling flaws. What he cared about was the town and the things that went on in it. From the window of our apartment we could see into the backyard of a family who kept chickens. Sherwood watched and observed and finally wrote a hilarious tale about a cat that fell in love with a chicken. They were, in fact, inseparable. Whenever we glanced out the window, the cat would be trailing after the chicken, nuzzling it and rubbing up against it. The chicken did not seem to mind but it was frustrating for both of them.

Sherwood invented a reporter named Buck Fever, who was described as a young lad from the hills who was "making it big" in the big city by coming to work for the *News* and the *Democrat*. Buck had various adventures with women and whiskey and had trouble with his hunting. He always shot the wrong thing and had a hunting dog who was too fast for him to keep up with.

Sherwood also invented a number of other characters that were connected to the paper in odd ways. A Mrs. Homing Pigeon was a genteel lady who was much concerned with culture and public affairs. There was a

Colonel Star Dust who worked in the bank and, of course, Al Jackson of the New Orleans swamps discovered there was a branch of the Jackson family tree growing right in Marion. Almost all of the poetry in the paper was written by Sherwood under the name of Jay G. Sigmund.

The townspeople of Marion loved all the odd characters Sherwood devised. They rarely read books and the weekly paper made up the bulk of their reading for the week. Sometimes Sherwood would kindle a minor crusade and sometimes the outcome was successful. There was, across from the printshop, a terribly dilapidated old building that housed the town's road equipment. Sherwood and Mrs. Homing Pigeon decreed that it was an eyesore and must go. Each week new articles would demand that the building be torn down and replaced by a pleasant park where people could sit in the sun and look at a tree. Finally the town capitulated and with a general sigh of relief the building went down. A park was laid out and Sherwood dubbed it the Henry Mencken Park in an editorial. But the town decided it was their new editor's park and named it Sherwood Forest. Later crusades were aimed at cleaning up the town jail, outfitting the town band and building a school for Negroes.

All during 1928, Sherwood and I worked together to put out the *News* and the *Democrat*. He gathered the news and wrote about it while I handled the business and correspondence for the two papers. I wrote checks to pay the bills and sometimes, when Sherwood went off to lecture in order to earn an extra hundred dollars, I would have to go down to the printshop to make sure that everybody got to work. I ordered type from time to time from a company that had always been reliable. I was surprised one day when they sent us the wrong kind of type. I wrote, asking them to correct the mistake and added: "You make so few errors that we count on you for accuracy." They wrote me a charming letter saying that no one had ever before apologized to them for their own error.

I was not as rapturously content to live in Marion as Sherwood seemed to be. There was no one to talk to for I did not have Sherwood's easy flair for making friends quickly. The women of the town were nice enough but very uninteresting and highly opinionated. Their church life was of paramount interest to them and I did not belong to a church, which upset them no end. There was an unspoken rule that on Sundays ladies wore hats and gloves, and I felt no pressing need to do so. I did not quite "fit in," and I had no intention of making myself over to conform to the town mold.

During that year we became acquainted with the Copenhaver clan. Mrs. Laura Lou Copenhaver was a dynamic and forceful woman who ran her family with the same energetic drive that she applied to business. Sherwood was very much taken with her and greatly enjoyed the long talks they had together. I had the feeling she was instructing him on the ways of the South and that he was eager for such education. Her husband, B. E., remained in the background of the family and seemed to me to be generally annoyed with everything around him.

The Copenhavers were the First Family of Marion and thus dictated the social and cultural life of the town. They often invited us to Sunday dinner and Sherwood would argue animatedly with Laura Lou about the Daughters of the American Revolution, to which she belonged, and they would discuss the Civil War and the Ways of the South. I rather resented the Copenhavers' cavalier disregard for the North and the way they half laughingly would refer to me as a damyankee. At one point I snapped, "You damn Southerners think you can say anything you like, don't you?"

But the Copenhavers put up with me for Sherwood's sake and Laura Lou once asked me to go to New York with her to help sell some blankets she had acquired. I had already learned that she had bought the entire output of a blanket factory. The blankets were machine-made but Laura Lou advertised them as if they had been woven by the gnarled hands of farm wives in tiny cottages.

I thought it smacked of sharp dealing myself but Sherwood admired her acumen.

I told Laura Lou that I would not be able to go to New York with her to sell blankets and she did not press the issue.

When we were alone, Sherwood asked me, "Why didn't you take her up on it? It was a good chance for you to see all your old friends in New York again. You let it go."

I said, "I let it go on purpose because she didn't want me anyway. All she wanted was your name to help sell those foolish blankets. If she had wanted my company all that badly she could have offered to pay my expenses and she didn't."

Sherwood shrugged. "Well, it was a chance that you let go."

"Well, it was a chance that I didn't want."

We left it at that, but I knew Sherwood was annoyed. He thought Laura Lou was a great woman and that it would have been good for me to accompany her, even though I would have had to buy new clothes for the trip.

It was near the end of 1928 when we met Laura Lou's daughter Eleanor, who had been in New York, working as the Industrial Secretary of the Young Women's Christian Association. One of her duties was to travel around the country to inspect the working conditions in the factories that were just then beginning to be affected by the general trend toward unionization.

Sherwood was feeling somewhat left out of things on a national level and wanted to know more about the labor agitation and the socialist movement. He began to feel that he had isolated himself unduly by living in a small town. Eleanor provided him with a link to the outside world which was changing so rapidly.

Robert had returned to Marion and was interesting himself in the workings of his father's newspapers. Sherwood had more time to think about the affairs of the country as a whole, for Robert had demonstrated a surprising talent for imitating his father's journalistic style.

In January of 1929, Sherwood told me we could probably afford a trip to California for me. I thought it was considerate of him, for it had been some years since I had seen my mother, and I decided to go. I also welcomed the change in climate, for California would be sunny and warm.

I arrived in California and enjoyed the family reunion and seeing my old friends there. Only a few days later, I received a familiar-looking letter and knew immediately that it was from Sherwood. I opened it, expecting one of his long, rambling letters about how he felt and what he thought.

Instead, he stated, quite simply, "I just wish you would not come back."

He gave no reasons and raised no issues. It was as though he were writing to an unwanted houseguest who had overstayed the welcome. My reaction to the letter was a cold, steady anger that consumed any love I still felt for Sherwood.

I burned his letters that I had kept for so long, along with the photographs I had of him, or Ripshin, or New Orleans. I dropped my wedding ring into a trash can. I set about to deliberately forget all I could of my marriage to Sherwood Anderson.

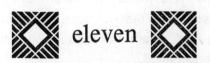 eleven

I never saw Sherwood again and received only a few letters from him, all having to do with the mechanics of separation. I had to reshape the substance of my life. I was forty-five years old then, and the prospect of settling into a routine job was drab. For that matter, in 1929 there was little employment even for younger women.

I was still looking for something which would fill my time when I got a letter from Sherwood asking if I would start proceedings for a divorce. I wrote back to tell him to do the dirty work himself. I had to live in California and I wanted no such scandal. He would have to do it all himself.

I have no idea where, or how, or, indeed, if he got the divorce. He never wrote me about it and I never received notification of it, but a few years later I read that he had married Eleanor Copenhaver. It was hardly a surprise to me, though I had a few qualms about never having received any divorce papers. Sherwood would have been perfectly capable of simply overlooking the fact of his previous marriage, but I did not think Eleanor was. Marrying Eleanor was a reasonable thing for Sherwood to do, I thought. He had always been romantic about the South and had created the legend that his father was a Southern man, though he had traveled in the South only while serving in the Ohio forces during the Civil War. The Copenhavers had seemed to Sherwood to personify the South and it is possible he believed the marriage would strengthen his own bond with the South.

About the time that Sherwood wrote, I received an odd letter from his son. The tone of the letter was almost accusing, as if Robert thought that it was I who had run out on Sherwood and him. Perhaps that is what he was led to believe. I answered him and tried to go back to living my own altered life.

My family would not allow that. Without telling me, Dorothea's husband Max and my brother David

wrote to Sherwood, saying that he should, in all con-
science, support me at least until I could find a suitable
job.

Sherwood wrote directly to me: "I know you didn't
have anything to do with this." It was quite true. I had
not, for I knew Sherwood had no money and no immediate prospect of making any.

In the course of time, David came home with the
news that the University of Stanford wanted to open up
a small bookstore. It was with a slight sense of shock
that I suddenly recalled I was a librarian and had considerable experience in running a bookshop.

The store did very well, but I still found that I had
more time on my hands than I cared to have. The Stanford library staff found out about this and asked if I
could order the books they needed. I agreed to do this
and they sent over their lists of books which I typed out
and sent to the appropriate companies.

It was a simple, undemanding life that provided me
with neither challenge nor interest. In my spare time I
began riding again. I wrote to Sherwood asking him to
send my riding boots and jodhpurs. While I was writing,
I recalled a lovely silver frame that belonged to me. I
had put a photograph of Sherwood in it. I asked for
that to be sent too, and told him he could remove his
photograph if he cared to.

Robert sent me the jodhpurs and boots, but not the frame. He included a brief, brisk note saying they had done their best and that was all they were going to do. I wondered about that for a time, then forgot it entirely.

At the bookstore, I met a wealthy doctor from Stanford who had a magnificent ranch. We became good friends and rode together frequently. His home was wonderfully rugged and rambling in the California style, with warm red Spanish tiles and stucco walls. The ranch itself was huge, dotted with almond trees that had an exquisite aroma when they bloomed. They were idyllic times, riding through orange groves under the clear blue bowl of the sky.

I had noticed the conspicuous absence of the doctor's wife, and one day he confided to me that he was separated from her and in the process of being divorced. It made me wonder about my own divorce, which seemed to be terribly slow in coming through.

Then the doctor asked me to marry him and it so surprised me that I was speechless for moments. Filled with the beauty of the countryside and the companionable pleasantness of his presence, I almost told him that I would marry him. Then I took a deep breath and reconsidered. I was not in love with the doctor; I was in love with the ranch. I would be marrying a hacienda and an orange grove and a herd of fine horses. The doctor was a mild and courtly man whose charm was partly derived from the fact that he was absolutely unstimulating. Very gently, I told him that I could not marry him.

We rode together less frequently after that and I concentrated more of my attention on the bookstore at Stanford. It took me little time to realize that my work would occupy my hours but that it could not occupy my life. Sherwood had been a sweeping force that had carried me along with him as long as I was with him. Now that I was not, I would have to provide my own impetus.

Oddly enough, it was Sherwood who helped me to find it. Unexpectedly, I received a letter from him with a check in it. When we were living at Ripshin, I had bought a pretty little farm on the top of a tiny hill for around four hundred dollars. Sherwood had built a small shack up there to have a place to go off and ruminate and write. The shack had windows all around so Sherwood could gaze out at the wild turkeys and the trees and he had been very fond of it. At the same time, Sherwood bought another small piece of land on the same hill. Now, he had apparently confused the two properties and thought that I owned them both.

He enclosed a check for six hundred dollars, which I showed to David and Stark Young, who was visiting us. Stark looked at me sharply. "You're not going to be fool enough to send it back, are you?"

"Well, I had thought about doing that."

David said, very firmly, "Of course you will keep it."

They were both very logical about the matter, listing the things that had been mine and were now Sherwood's. In the end I decided to keep the money.

For no real reason, I wanted to use the money to see Mexico. Natalie Scott, the very social columnist for the *Times-Picayune*, had written to me, inviting me to visit her in Taxco, a small town about eighty miles south of Mexico City. I had always liked Natalie and she had been more my friend than Sherwood's, which may have been a deciding factor in accepting her invitation.

I announced to my startled family that I was taking a trip into Mexico for an indefinite stay. At first they were worried that Sherwood's wanderlust might have rubbed off on me, but then they decided it would be an interesting thing for me to do. I found a small book of basic Spanish phrases and went off to what was, in 1931, a rough, unsettled and adventuresome country.

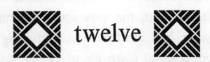 **twelve**

Juárez, a hot and dusty cluster of slapped-up shacks and crumbling adobe huts, had nothing to recommend it. I looked at the bus station and quickly decided to take the train. The buses were unthinkable — ancient, towering wrecks that wheezed and clanked, piled impossibly high with baskets, boxes, serapes and battered black trunks. The buses were jammed beyond capacity with poor Mexicans who seemed not to mind competing for living space with pigs, geese and several bunches of live chickens, tied together at the feet and hanging head down, like feathery bouquets.

The train station was slightly better and I looked for

the window marked *"Primera Clase."* Because I spoke no Spanish I had trouble explaining what I wanted, but I finally managed by pointing to the sign overhead and then to Mexico City on the tattered map behind the clerk.

The train was marvelous — a big, black, noisy, spitting, hissing, clanking hulk that was pockmarked with what I instantly took for bullet scars, for I had read that the Mexican Revolution had been one of the few wars to tactically employ trains. To my considerable delight, there was a uniformed armed guard in each passenger car.

I boarded the train and it started off with a billowing cloud of white steam and a shower of hot cinders. Soon we were clicking along through a barren, arid desert that was unrelieved by the few cacti that dotted it. The heat waves rippling from the baked ground seemed to dissolve the horizon, as though the desert simply melted into the burning sky. The only excitement of the trip existed in the landscape of my mind, which was peopled with bandits and outlaws and murderous rebels. They did not materialize. The train simply kept moving along, with so little variety in the scenery that it might have been on a huge treadmill. From time to time, vendors would pass through the train, selling *tortas*, which are hard-crusted rolls filled with a dubious assortment of wilted vegetables and meats. I ate them with good appetite and many misgivings.

Then the countryside changed, and even the slumped guard stood up straighter. We passed small rippling streams and waterfalls, flowering trees and fields of neatly aligned maguey cacti. I later learned that the maguey cacti were as carefully tended as cows, for a farmer with a good "herd" of maguey could expect excellent returns. The milk of the maguey can be fed to infants and is called *agua de miel*; fermented, the milk becomes *pulque*; distilled, it becomes *mescal* or *tequila*.

The tracks of the train no longer cut across the naked skin of the desert like a straight, raw scar, but gently conformed to the contours of the land, winding and dipping and rising, and with every curve I saw new green marvels. This was the Mexico I had wanted to find.

Along the tracks, children popped up unexpectedly to wave at the train, as children do everywhere, but here there were no visible houses or villages. Always, the children were accompanied by dogs, and I gradually became aware of a singular oddity. In each village we passed through, there was a dominant breed of dog, with almost no variations. One village would have dogs that were all black, another would have all tan, or all russet, dogs. It seemed that the dogs were owned communally and allowed to breed as freely as they wandered in the dusty streets. The dogs were treated with a casual cruelty that shocked me. I saw one small girl with large, liquid black eyes and a cherubic face, flailing away at the pitifully prominent ribs of an underfed dog. It made me realize, even more than the strange, sibilant language, how alien I was to this country.

People I met on the train were invariably courteous to me, but I knew that there was a general, if unspoken, curiosity about a woman traveling alone. I managed to indicate my needs with the Spanish phrase book and many elaborate gestures which they were patient enough to interpret.

Then the train stopped in a small town and simply stayed there. I wondered why until the conductor managed to make me understand that it would not be leaving until the next day. Fortunately, the Spanish word for "hotel" is "hotel" and I found it and checked in. It was a Saturday and that night I heard what was to become a familiar sound in my life — the village band. The make-up of such bands differs according to the locale. In the north of Mexico there are the *mariaches*, loud, shrill cornets, brassy trumpets and guitars. In the south, near Oaxaca and Tehuantepec, *marimbas* dominate the musical scene, with their peculiar, bubbling sound. Around Vera Cruz, harps and guitars are used to play the rapid, agitated music of the region. Mostly the musicians are untrained and inexpert, but they play with such an enthusiastic verve that it is contagious and delightful, if not continued too long.

In this village, the band's enthusiasm was matched by their perseverance and the music blared on late into the night. The loud, walloping boom of the bass drum seemed to control the throbbing in my head as I lay on the straw-stuffed mattress, staring up at the whitewashed adobe ceiling. When the raucous racket finally stopped, so did consciousness. I fell asleep at once.

The journey to Mexico City took days and days but it was not monotonous. Always, the scenery was novel and beautiful and there were always incidents to be amused by, shocked at, or pleased with. It was a dangerous time to be in Mexico, for there was great general discontent with the President, who was Ortiz Rubio and was said to be a mere puppet of former President Calles, who lived in Cuernavaca on what was called the "Street of Forty Thieves," and who controlled the government. But at the time I was aware of none of this. I may have seen *politicos* haranguing a group of Indians on a corner, but I understood not a word. There may have been flurries of political protest activity, even on the train itself, but I noticed none of them.

During the long stops in the larger towns, I looked at the store windows, fascinated with what I found, things such as great, garish cakes to commemorate any occasion at all — even major surgery, for I saw one cake topped with an operating table and four candy surgeons grouped around a sugar patient, complete with tiny rivulets of frosting blood. In all towns, large or small, there were displays of native crafts on the sidewalks and in storefronts. The pottery had infinite variety in color and shape; no piece like any other, by design and not by faulty workmanship.

The train moved into the mountains, climbing higher and higher, and I marveled at the dogged persistence of the farmers who planted fields of corn on the sides of steep inclines that seemed almost vertical. How did they manage to keep their plow in the ground and not go tumbling along with it into the steeper ravines below? And why did they keep on farming this rugged, mountainous country? Why not move — burro, bundles and babies — into a flatter, kinder area? It was a long time before I learned the kind of attachment that a Mexican can have for his own land — his *tierra*.

When I finally arrived in Mexico City I was in a strange state of exhaustion from the trip and exhilaration from the wonderful new things I had seen and done. I had a few names of Americans living in Mexico City, given to me by a friend in California, so I called some of them and learned where to live and how.

I rented a small apartment in a large colonial style house. It had a tiny kitchen, a living room and a bedroom and was located in the Colonial Roma, near the main shopping area and the Paseo de la Reforma, which I soon decided was the loveliest boulevard I had ever seen. It was divided by a broad, green lawn with great, towering trees. It began in the heart of the city and ran for miles through the residential area of the wealthy.

At intervals along the Reforma, there were statues — a soaring obelisk topped by a floodlit golden angel, a graceful Diana amid a showering spray of lighted water from a fountain, and many others. To one side of the Reforma was Chapultepec Park, a handsome place of fine shade trees and meandering paths that led inevitably to the small lake in its center. On Sundays, I strolled with the rest of the populace through the park, marveling at how very much it was enjoyed by the people who brought their children for picnics. Mexican fathers seemed to me to be extraordinarily doting with their children. I knew they worked long and hard during the week to eke out a living. The weekends were, perhaps, the only times they had to see their offspring.

I resolved to take Spanish lessons but I kept putting

it off because there was so much to do and see. I had not yet contacted Natalie Scott for the same reasons. She did not even know I was in Mexico. I thought about writing her and casually looked for the address, but could not find it. Most likely I had not been given an address other than simply Taxco and had not written it down. There was no great concern. I would find Natalie later.

I met Katherine Anne Porter through a letter to her that had been written by a young man I knew at Stanford. Katherine Anne had been deeply involved in the Revolution for some years before I met her. Some said she had even been active in it, but I think she simply knew all the people who were fighting in it. They were all friends together, the leaders of the Revolution and many artists and writers. This was at a time when alliances and loyalties were in a state of flux. The influential person who was your friend a week before might no longer be in good standing with the Powers, and if you retained your friendship, your own standing might be suspect. Katherine Anne, of course, had a great many friends who were controversial, and because of that the current Powers did not care for her. No matter. In a month, the situation would be changed.

Katherine Anne was very popular with her friends, however, and she had many of them. She had a dark prettiness and was a strange, complicated girl who could be perfectly charming or perfectly horrible with no apparent reason for either extreme. She lived in a funny old house near the Lagunilla Market and could neither cook nor clean house, but she could write. Her house, it seemed to me, was uncomfortable and almost devoid of furniture, but Katherine Anne did not mind at all sitting on uncarpeted floors. She had a small room in which she wrote, with a window facing a blank wall, and this satisfied her nicely.

I was not introduced to the young man who also lived in the house so I never knew if he was her husband or not, but he was considerably younger than Katherine Anne. I decided there was probably no formal relation between them when he abruptly disappeared, having been summarily ordered out, according to Katherine Anne's friends.

In the evenings, she had a succession of youngish men who admired her and who took her out constantly. I was told by her friends, who told entirely too many stories it seemed to me, that Katherine Anne had once received a prize of five hundred dollars for something she had written. She went to the bank with the money order and was given the money in gold pieces, as was the custom then for American money. It was handed over to her in the regular white canvas bag and she took it with her on her regular round of seeing people and meeting friends. Before the day was over, she had lost the heavy sack and it was never found. In those days, a person could live for months and months on that much money.

I had been in Mexico City for perhaps two months when I went out to pick up some groceries and met, on the street, Bill Spratling. I had not seen him since I lived in New Orleans and had completely forgotten that he had moved to Mexico to live. Natalie Scott had mentioned it in her letter and I was again reminded that I had done nothing about seeing her in Taxco. Bill and I went back to my apartment to talk about old times and new ones.

When Bill said that he had been sorry to hear about "that business with Sherwood," I was surprised for an instant. I had been so completely involved in my new surroundings that I had put him out of my mind almost entirely. The sound of his name came as a small shock. I explained what had happened and we went on to talk of happier things.

Bill had moved to Mexico in 1929, ostensibly to write a book called *Little Mexico*, but, as it turned out, to become involved in the silver industry in Taxco, where Natalie lived. The town had always been a silver mining center in Mexico, even in the days of the Aztecs. When Bill moved there he decided it would be a good thing for the town and the Indians if they were to utilize the silver they mined, rather than to ship it elsewhere to be made into jewelry. He set up a shop in which he taught a few talented natives how to work the silver into the ingenious designs he created. These natives taught others, and by the time I saw Bill in Mexico it was a solidly established business.

It seemed to me that Bill was far more lively and self-assertive than he had been in New Orleans where he was overshadowed by the forceful personalities of Sherwood and Bill Faulkner. Now, in Mexico, he had come into his own. He had just finished *Little Mexico*, he told me, and was about to ship it off to his publisher.

Later that morning, Bill introduced me to Daniel Rubin de la Borbolla, who was studying at the University of Mexico to become a doctor. Some years later, he founded the Museum of Popular Arts instead. It was a fascinating place, with all the best arts and crafts of Mexico sold there. Later he went on to become the Director of the National Museum and a highly respected anthropologist.

But when I met him that day, he was a young student with a day off from his studies. He said, "Bill and I are going to drive over to Puebla and Cholula — come along."

The drive seemed to take forever, but none of us

minded. Bill told me all about his adopted town of Taxco
and convinced me that I would have to go back with
him when he returned. Daniel, even then, was an authority on the native crafts of his country, and his enthusiasm
was contagious.

The road was twisting and devious and Bill drove as
though possessed, chattering and glancing over his
shoulder at Daniel and me, then turning his attention
briefly to the road. Finally I reminded him that we were
on a leisurely country drive, not a Grand Prix, and he
compromised the speed of the car for a time.

Puebla, when we finally reached it, proved to be a
city of old colonial buildings and was the central market-
ing place for the region. Daniel loaded up the car with
black, shiny ceramics from Oaxaca and lovely blue and
white tiles from Puebla.

Later we went to Cholula, which was an astonishing
place. In the days before the Spaniards came to Mexico,
Cholula had been a religious center of great importance.
There had been countless pyramids and temples and the
Spaniards had razed them all. In their place, churches
had been erected until the entire countryside was littered
with churches. Wherever I looked I could see dozens of
church domes of every description. Some of them
sparkled gold in the late afternoon sun and others were

blue and pink and checkered or weathered gray by the years. There were domes and spires, steeples, turrets, minarets and cupolas.

I looked at Daniel and Bill helplessly. "It's quite a sight," was all I could say.

Bill's angular, jutting jaw went tense and he looked around grimly. "It is, when you think about what the natives live in around the churches," he said.

The area was a city of churches with no one to live in them but plaster and wooden saints. The natives lived in adobe and stone huts, squalid next to the baroque grandeur of the churches. There was, Daniel informed me, a church for every day of the year. The churches were desolate and empty for the entire year, used only when the patron saint of a particular church had his "day."

When we looked more closely at a few of the churches, it became apparent that the Catholic Church had never completely subdued the Aztecs. Daniel pointed out to me the symbolism of the ancient Aztec gods that had been worked into the intricate designs on the outside of the church. Each of the saints had a counterpart in the architecture and design of the structures. The church for St. John the Baptist, for example, would contain the symbols for the ancient god of rain, Tlaloc. Thus, when the natives celebrated St. John the Baptist's "day," they would also be silently and privately commemorating the venerable Tlaloc.

At least there is that, I thought to myself. Each church had been built upon the destroyed ruins of a pyramid or temple, but like the phoenix, the desecrated god of the past had risen along with the new church.

The spectacle of the gleaming churches was beautiful and appalling and I was glad when we finally trooped back to the car and drove back to Puebla.

We stayed overnight in the least miserable hotel we could find. I could not even try to imagine the conditions that must prevail in the other hotels. This one was impossible. The rooms were vast, with cold tile floors and absurdly tall ceilings. It was like sleeping in a huge, deserted depot. The thick concrete walls sweated, the plumbing groaned and clattered from the coldness of the water, and room service was a luxury of the future.

Bill and Daniel and I met downstairs in an open-air cafe, each of us filled with recriminations about our accommodations. We looked at each other's tight-lipped, grumpy expressions and, without a word being exchanged, burst into laughter. Hardships shared can be a source of hilarity.

The food, at any rate, was first-class. I allowed myself to be persuaded to sample the *mole poblano*, a local specialty that had long ago been invented by a nun to

honor a visiting dignitary of the church. It was a generous serving of turkey, swimming in a rich hot sauce
made with chocolate, tomatoes and many varieties of
chili. The flavor of it was absolutely alien to my palate,
but very delicious.

We sat in the sidewalk cafe until late, alternately
reminiscing and talking with enthusiasm of the future,
which is one of the most satisfying conversations it is
possible to have. Bill and Daniel drank tequila in the
classic way, with lemon and salt: a wedge of lemon is
sucked to clear the palate, the tequila is downed in a
gulp, and then the salt is sprinkled on the back of the
hand, at the juncture of the thumb and forefinger; the
wrist is smartly rapped with the other hand and the salt
leaps into the open mouth, deadening the bite of the
tequila. I contented myself with lemonade, for it is an
operation that cannot be properly performed by a
woman.

Very late, we parted and went to our sleeping de-
pots, tired enough to sleep even on the unyielding pallets that passed as beds.

In the morning I was introduced to the Mexican
breakfast, which is totally unlike all others — the crisp,
flaky croissants and café of Paris; the heavy, perhaps
indigestible spreads of England; the spartan servings of
bacon and eggs in the Midwest; or the spicy concoctions

of New Orleans. Here I was served — at Bill's insistence — *huevos rancheros*: toasted tortillas covered by fried eggs and then with a piquant sauce of onions, tomatoes and chilis. The waiter also approached with two carafes and simultaneously poured into a large glass scalded milk and black, strong, boiled coffee — *café con leche*.

We drove back to Mexico City with Bill making exuberant and peremptory plans for my immediate future as we went. He insisted that I pack all my belongings and leave my apartment so that I could go with him to Taxco. I was surprised to find that I did not resent being taken in tow that way. It seemed that I had no direction in mind and was willing to be diverted into any channel that looked promising.

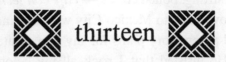 **thirteen**

Bill drove me, a willing captive, out of Mexico City, past the University of Mexico to the road leading to Cuernavaca. There had been an early morning shower which gave a washed radiance to the world. A jacaranda tree had shed its lavender petals on the black asphalt and the beauty of the contrast was almost electric.

We climbed high into the mountains and, looking back, I saw Mexico City, stretched out like a patchwork quilt over the valley. At an altitude of around ten thousand feet, we stopped going up and began the descent to Cuernavaca; the road swooped and curved along the way. At one point we raced alongside a little steam engine which ran along on narrow-gauge tracks and chugged manfully on the inclines. We left it behind to meander its leisurely route to Cuernavaca. At certain bends in the road I caught brief glimpses of the little town in the valley far below. Then there was a long, graceful curve around the foot of the mountain and the road leveled out into Cuernavaca.

It was a lush and lovely town with flowers spilling over pink adobe walls like waterfalls and trees that were huge bouquets of flowers. As we drove down a narrow street, I could see through long grilled windows to the patios inside, filled with flowers and birds on brilliant green lawns. All the houses had been gaily painted and the sun had softened them to pastel shades of green and pink and blue.

Bill showed me the cathedral, a massive and severe building that the Franciscans had built in 1529. The stern, heavy walls accommodated bright splashes of bougainvillea that tumbled over them.

Bill was pleased with my ecstatic reaction to "his" country; he announced that we would stop for lunch at the Hotel Marik-Plaza. We made our way to the patio that overlooked the town plaza and sat sipping drinks and admiring the laurel trees, with their dark green densely grown leaves that shaded the tiny square.

After lunch we drove out of town on a road lined with mango and papaya trees and sprawling elephant

213

ears and rubbery tropical plants. We were heading for the *tierra caliente*, the warm lands of the state of Guerrero. We passed waterfalls and a stream that seemed to run backwards, away from the ocean, as it crossed and recrossed the road. I sat back in the car seat and silently marveled at the scenery, which was consistently stunning. There was no way for me to talk about my reaction to what I saw and Bill seemed to appreciate this.

We began climbing a mountain and Bill told me that Taxco was on the other side of it. We rounded a turn where a waterfall had cut its way down the green mountainside to fall in a feathery plume to the pool below, and I saw Taxco for the first time.

It was a town like no other. It was cupped into the side of the mountain, round and concave in contour. The houses and buildings were all of a pattern, soft pastel greens and pinks and yellows that blended together as if everyone who lived there had agreed not to build anything that might mar the effect. As a result, the town had an entity to which everything in it contributed — the cobblestoned winding streets, the red-tiled roofs, and the flowers and green tropical plants. In the center of the cup, the huge, rococo parish church of Santa Prisca dominated the small plaza as it did the whole town.

Bill's car grumbled up the alarmingly steep street, barely wide enough for a single car. I wondered about the protocol if we should happen to meet another car coming the opposite way, for one of the cars would have to retreat a considerable distance. The problem never came up, however, and we labored up a final hill and came out on the Borda Plaza, beneath the great church. Here, Bill parked.

"Do you live here?" I asked, looking around and seeing only a few shops and walls.

"No, but this is as close as we can drive," he said cheerfully, getting out of the car and unloading my luggage and his own. At once, he was surrounded by chattering children, all eager to carry the luggage of Don Guillermo and his guest. He selected several of the sturdiest and they snatched up the parcels and suitcases and went racing up the almost vertical cobblestone lane. Bill did not seem worried about the possibility of theft so I decided I could not be either.

As we stood in the road, we were hailed from a balcony overlooking the plaza and facing the church. It was the Bar Paco and it was Natalie Scott who was waving at us. We waved back and headed for the bar.

After a feverish flurry of greetings, I was able to take a good look at Natalie. She had not changed at all from the time I had known her in New Orleans. She was still a big, strapping woman who tended toward flamboyant dress and exuberant manner. Now she carried, no, flourished, a flaming red parasol and wore the kind of crisply ruffled, curiously mismatched clothes that had come to be associated with her.

We all sat down at a table, ordered something to drink, and Natalie started talking, dominating the conversation by sheer drive and vitality. Her great booming laughter rolled out over the plaza and made the natives look up to the Bar Paco curiously.

Natalie had come to Taxco in 1930. She told me she had come on horseback from Brownsville and that a local legend had grown up around her fantastic trip of over eight hundred miles through wild territory. Everyone in Taxco believed that she had come riding triumphantly into the Borda Plaza and that her horse had promptly dropped dead of sheer exhaustion. It was a legend I would not find hard to believe, considering her sturdy frame. I asked her if it was true.

"Of course not!" she said. "Not more than two weeks after I got here, Caroline Durieux and I wanted to go see an old hacienda in the country. Caroline offered to supply me with a horse but I said, 'That's foolish. I've got a perfectly good horse that I rode here from Brownsville.'

"So I had the horse saddled and brought out. It took one long, sad look at me. *That's* when it dropped dead!"

Natalie rocked with laughter. "The poor thing thought I was heading back to the border!"

At that point the bells of Santa Prisca began to ring, as if in salute to the legend of Natalie's horse. Bill glanced at his watch and shouted, over the clanging of the bells, "We'll go on up to my house and have dinner."

"Fine!" Natalie roared back. We got up and left the bar. At the other end of the plaza we turned into a lane so narrow that we had to walk single file. This became even narrower after a short climb and I could touch the wall on both sides of me. I was wearing city shoes that did not easily accommodate to the slippery, loose cobblestones, and the lane was as steep as a staircase.

"You get used to climbing here in Taxco," Bill commented, not even out of breath.

When we came to a slightly wider street named Calle de las Delicias, Bill unlocked a door and then stepped back with a grand flourish to allow us to enter. Inside was a carefully executed jungle, with lemon and orange trees, *wispero*, laurel, roses and a great many trees and plants I could not then identify. Bill led us over a flagstone path to a spacious living room with handcrafted leather and wood chairs and a massive wooden table. It was very clearly a man's home.

"Tonyoo!" Bill called out in a way that was to become familiar to me. At once, a Mexican houseboy appeared with a bucket of ice, a variety of bottles and several glasses on a tray. He set the tray down on the table and was about to slip away when Bill stopped him. In Spanish, he introduced me as "La Señora Anderson."

When the boy had gone, Bill told me that Antonio (which was the "Tonyoo" he had shouted) had not been able to make it as a silversmith but had become a first-class majordomo. Bill had established a good-natured camaraderie with his workers that consisted of mutual affection and respect.

We talked quietly in the slowly darkening *sala*, until Antonio decreed it was time for dinner, by quietly serving it.

After dinner, Natalie peered at me, then said, "Why, you poor thing, you must be exhausted. We'll go right over to my place and get you into bed." She turned to Bill. "You can have one of your boys take her luggage across, can't you?"

"Well, she can stay right here if she wants to . . ." Bill began, but Natalie cut him off.

"Absolutely not. What would people say? Anyway, this big old drafty place is only fit for dogs and menfolk. We'll just trot her right across the barranca where she can be comfortable."

Natalie was already on her feet and bustling about. I

allowed myself to be led out of Bill's house and down a steep stone staircase. At the foot of the stairs there appeared to be an impenetrable jungle, which we promptly penetrated. Natalie's house was separated from Bill's by a deep ravine, or barranca. Now, Natalie took my hand and led me into the jungle along a path I could not see. I heard the chattering of wild animals nearby and the muted hooting of owls in the night. Then we came to another set of stone stairs, which we climbed.

Natalie's house was furnished frivolously but comfortably. Almost the instant we arrived, a massive knocker on the front door sounded and a cluster of people spilled into the house. Natalie greeted them all gaily and introduced me around. I made no effort to record their names on my mind, for more people were streaming in and more introductions were being made.

Everyone had drinks in short order and somebody had a fiddle. Soon the party was going full sway. I sat in an easy chair at one side of the room and watched it. Music and talk swirled like smoke around the room, ice cubes clinked, a glass crashed, a woman laughed, high and shrill . . . I nodded off.

I was wakened by a shriek of dismay. It was Natalie. She stood over me solicitously and made a great, grand show of hustling me off to bed.

In the darkened room, I lay in bed listening to the

219

roar of the party that sounded like several jukeboxes gone mad, playing backwards. I slept.

Sunlight formed a bright yellow square on the bed. I lay there for a while, looking around at the clean white walls, the few gaily colored paintings, the dark red tile floors. Through the open window I heard the shrill yapping of dogs and the sound of people calling out to each other from across the barranca. Somewhere, someone began pounding something. Suddenly a great pealing of the bells of Santa Prisca jolted me upright. I glanced at my watch. Six-thirty. Life began early in Taxco.

My clothes had been neatly stored in a dresser and hung in a small closet. On a table were a large basin, a pitcher of water and several glasses. I washed, then got dressed and went quietly out to see if anyone else was up.

Natalie was sitting out on the patio in a ruffly pink peignoir. "Good morning," she said, then waved to someone across the barranca.

"Good morning," I said. She poured coffee for me and then a maid quickly brought in breakfast. "I had expected Taxco to be a quiet little town," I remarked casually.

"Not a bit," she said. "Noise all the time. When it's not the bells or the dogs it's the skyrockets or the fiestas down on the plaza. Taxco's no place to be if you can't stand a little noise."

"I don't really mind it," I admitted. "It's just different."

We sat in the sun over coffee, neither of us feeling any need to make small talk. Finally Natalie got to her feet. "Did you bring riding clothes?" she asked.

"I did, as a matter of fact. I just haven't had a chance to use them yet."

"Today's your chance. Why don't we both change and then go for a long ride. It'll give you a good look at some of the country around here."

The horses were in fine fettle and we jogged along comfortably over rolling hills and sloping pastures. A line from a long-forgotten poem insinuated itself into my mind: ". . . a green thought in a green shade." It was what I felt.

We rode for hours and returned to Natalie's house in time for a late lunch, after which, as was the custom in Mexico, we retired for a siesta.

That night, Natalie announced: "Everybody's coming tonight."

"Everybody?" I echoed, somewhat apprehensively.

"Yes," she replied decisively. "They all want to meet you."

And everybody, indeed, did come over that night. All of Taxco seemed to be flowing in and out of the house. People sat in chairs and on the floors. The party spilled up on the roof and out on the patio. Couples danced or stood around chatting and drinking.

It was an exciting time and I laughed and talked with more animation than I had felt in many months. The plumber came in. Someone told me he was a very bad plumber but a very good dancer. He invited me to dance and I was whirled around the room until properly dizzy. The plumber was great fun, even though we spoke different languages, but finally I realized that he was calling me Señorita Natalie. It confused me, for I looked nothing at all like Natalie. I asked a bilingual bystander to solve the mystery. There was a brief exchange and my translator reported: "He says all Americans look alike to him."

I had often heard Americans say that all Chinese looked alike to them. It was strange being in a country in which I looked like all other Americans to a Mexican. I liked the idea and went on dancing with the plumber, who went on calling me Señorita Natalie.

That night I met a myriad of tourists and U.S. residents and natives and I even managed to retain the names of a few. Taxco was just beginning to be discovered by tourists, mostly because of Bill Spratling's budding silver industry. It was a good and inexpensive place for struggling artists and starving writers to live and nearly everyone I met was doing something that seemed very important to him or her. That made it a fine town, in my eyes. There are places in Mexico — Puerta Vallarta used to be one of them — where artists come to vegetate and writers come to stagnate. They lie in hammocks sipping endlessly at drinks and languidly creating great art, but only in their muddled minds. Some places reek of this brand of decadence and it is easy to be lulled into the soporific stasis that is their life.

But Taxco was not such a place. The artists I met were working ones and sometimes even selling ones. Bill was simultaneously writing *Little Mexico* and creating jewelry designs to be painstakingly worked into fine silver. Caroline Durieux was working hard at paintings that would later be shown at the Museum of Modern Art. Donald Cordray was collecting and studying the native crafts in Guerrero and Tamara Schee had a ballet school. Even Natalie Scott was writing a book about her quite fabulous life. She never did finish it, but she worked on it furiously, writing in a scrawled hand that was illegible, even to her. She made notes constantly and shuffled them around until they were hopelessly scrambled, and she would have to spend an entire day trying to find out where, exactly, she was in the story of her life. By the time she had gotten her notes in order, she was too exhausted to do anything but throw a party.

Taxco was no sleepy little town in the sun; an air of vitality and purpose permeated everything. Even at the parties, people set out to have a good time and did so with great gusto.

Finally, though, I had to return to California. There were things to do and decisions I had to make. The only painting I brought back with me was one that had been done by David Siqueiros, who was then in jail for some political offense. Frances Toor showed me the painting and told me it was his latest one. I liked it enormously. It was a painting of the artist himself, standing with the prison bars behind him, with two women who looked like angels in pale-colored rebozos and a small child in white, all holding out their hands to him. His face, in the painting, was anguished, as though he were suffering because he had nothing to give them.

Siqueiros, at that time, had a notion that he would like to be a Renaissance man and mix his paints from natural materials. For this one, he used a mixture of honey and varnish and other unlikely ingredients.

When I arrived in California, my sister Margaret saw the painting and immediately asked if she could use it for an exhibit of modern art at Mills College. I agreed, and then forgot about the painting until some time later Margaret came to me in an excited and distraught state.

The painting was ruined, she told me in a shocked whisper.

"Ruined? How was it ruined?" I asked her.

"I don't know. Just look at it."

Astonishingly, the painting had eroded. I could not imagine why until I finally recalled what Frances Toor had told me about the ingredients in the paint. Ants, it seemed, had found their way to the honey and had eaten their way through it, completely destroying the painting, except for those areas which were unsweetened by honey.

I assured Margaret that it could not possibly be her fault or the fault of Mills College. I could only hope that Siqueiros would find another aspect of the Renaissance to emulate.

I remained in California for a time, but life seemed curiously flat after Mexico. People took buses to work all at the same time, and the parties I went to were dignified affairs at which people exchanged solemn views. Sidewalks were uninteresting after cobblestones. No wild, clamorous bells assailed the senses. The sky was never attacked by explosive skyrockets.

I knew, without coming to any conscious decision

about it, that I would return to live in Taxco. The family estate, it developed, would be able to supply me with one hundred and fifty dollars a month, with which I would be able to live comfortably in Taxco. I would find something to do, for I knew I could not be content without some kind of work to keep me occupied. I was surprised and pleased when my family agreed that Taxco might be a good place for me. Perhaps my enthusiasm had reached them.

I made all the final arrangements. I packed things, shipped boxes off, arranged for a passport, bought tickets, and finally I was on my way back to my green thought in a green shade.

 fourteen

In Taxco, none of us were young, but we felt young and we behaved young. There was a rebirth of youthful enthusiasm and we felt that valuable things could be done in this vibrant country that was still shuddering from a violent and bloody revolution.

We wanted to impart the quality and intensity of Mexico to our lives and our work. Bill Spratling incorporated early pre-Columbian designs into his silver in a highly distinctive way. Natalie Scott went on long and arduous horseback rides with Donald Cordray, who was collecting native art for one of the museums in New York. Once they went all the way to Michoacán and ended up in Acapulco, stopping in villages to buy up

227

native crafts such as embroideries, pottery and children's toys. Donald and Natalie engaged in a continuous but good-natured argument over which of them had grabbed up all the best items.

Once, I was awakened in the middle of the night by one of the housemaids who told me that Donald Cordray needed me. "Tell Elizabeth to come quickly!" was what he had said.

I swiftly threw on a robe, certain that something terrible had happened to Donald and that he was calling for me to help him. I followed the maid out into the *sala*. Donald was stretched out in an easy chair, with his arms dangling loosely over the sides.

"For heaven's sakes, Donald, what is it?" I asked in alarm.

He looked at me with glazed eyes. "Coffee," was all that he could say. This was after one of Natalie's protracted parties and I knew that Donald did not drink very much. It took very little to "do him in" and clearly it had been done.

I hurried to make him a pot of coffee, then filled him up with enough of the steaming brew so that he could sit up, then walk around for a while, and finally make his way home.

Natalie was a marvel. She had a seemingly endless store of energy and could ride all day over hills and rocky roads, sleep on a floor somewhere, and then get up in the morning and do it all over again. We were all sure that nothing in the world could stop Natalie, but a few amoebas nearly did. She had bad attacks of dysentery but refused to do anything about them until it was almost too late. Then she took the cure. The cure consisted of being fed a poison that, if it did not kill you, would kill your amoebas.

For a few days, Natalie staggered around weakly and then set about recuperating. She galloped pell-mell down the road to recovery and was soon in full cry again.

At times Natalie's parties became unruly. High spirits carried to extremes can become hysteria. At one party people were unusually gay and abandoned, scuttling about for drinks, dancing flamenco, roaring dirty jokes to each other and urging people on to wilder behavior. In the early morning the party overflowed to the roof from the sheer press of people. Then, with the abruptness of an ax stroke, everything stopped short.

Someone had fallen off the roof. In seconds, rumors began to whistle like bullets through the air. She was dead, mangled, had been pushed, no, thrown — it was Natalie, no, Elizabeth . . .

Cooler heads prevailed, however, and a doctor was summoned. The calming order of facts was restored. A young girl had fallen off the edge of the roof and had broken her arm on the cobblestones below. The arm was being set and no permanent damage had been done. The party could end now.

Tamara Schee was also living in Taxco with her husband Kim, who was writing his book *Cantina*. Tamara had been a protégé of Pavlova, the great dancer who once had a house near Washington Square where she housed a flock of little girls of six or seven. She fed and clothed and housed them and taught them to dance. When I lived in New York, I had seen her several times with her flock of girls in tow. All the children wore pale woolen leggings and French blue coats and were all very gifted. Tamara had somehow been cut off from her family when her father went off to some distant land and had failed to send for her. Pavlova took her in and raised her.

Now Tamara lived in Taxco, after teaching dancing for some years in St. Louis. She was oddly cosmopolitan for Taxco and called everyone "darling," even the Mexicans, who could not possibly have understood the casual endearment.

Tamara and Kim were both passionate advocates of free love and other burning issues of the day, but in point of fact, were both in love with each other. It made their side affairs awkward because the left-out partner would become so jealous they found it impossible to live with their ideals. Tamara had a small school of dancing and had learned to massage dancers. Her business prospered and she hired a girl to help her. Her husband inconveniently found himself irresistibly drawn to the new girl and soon ran off with her. Then he ran out of money and was forced to send word to Tamara to come and rescue him and the girl. It developed into a strange ménage.

Tamara and I went riding around Taxco very often, sometimes with Natalie Scott and other times with people who came to visit Natalie. One such person was an English girl named Beatrice whose husband had stayed behind in Mexico City. We took her out for a ride which ended in a torrential downpour, and we returned drenched. We all changed clothes at Natalie's place, then started to walk over to Bill's house, where we had been invited to dinner. Beatrice suddenly remembered something she had to do and rushed off. Tamara and I went on to Bill's house and told him he might have to hold dinner for a while because Beatrice would be late.

Bill frowned darkly. He hated having his schedule disrupted. "That's very inconvenient," he snapped. "We can't do it."

"You'll have to, because she'll be showing up here expecting dinner," I told him. We sat out on his patio, having a few more drinks than we would ordinarily have had. An hour late, Beatrice showed up.

Bill had prepared himself to despise her, but Beatrice had a dazzling smile and bright yellow, curly hair. She overwhelmed Bill's black mood and after dinner, when she produced from her purse a long black cigar which she lit up, Bill was completely charmed.

At about ten-thirty that night, Tamara and I were dying to end the party and go home but Bill was still fascinated. Finally Beatrice said, "Well, I'll have to be getting back to Mexico City, I suppose."

Startled, I said, "You can't go back now. There isn't any way to get there."

"Oh yes," she said, "There's an eleven-o'clock bus to Mexico City."

I said, "My dear, I'm *sure* there isn't. I never heard of it."

Quite unconcerned, she said, "Well, I'm positive there is. If you'll just take me down there, I'll be able to find it."

I gave up. She could not be convinced, so Tamara and I led her down in the dark to the bus stop. "This is where the bus comes, isn't it?" she asked, as confident as ever.

"*When* the bus comes," I said.

She sat down on a bench to wait. Her yellow hair,

with a large diamond clip in it, gleamed in the street-
light directly over her head. She was a strange sight in
the almost deserted street and a traffic policeman who
was just going off duty asked me, "Where is her husband?"

I shrugged helplessly. "You'll just have to take care
of her. Her husband is in Mexico City and she's determined to get back to him tonight. She insists there's a
bus."

He looked at me and shrugged just as helplessly.

We left her there, sitting in a bright circle of light,
as if she were a spotlighted ballerina onstage, about to
move slowly into her dance.

At about midnight, I heard her enter Natalie's house
and settle down for the night on the couch. In the morning she was fresh as a daffodil and said not a word about
late-night buses to Mexico City. Was this, I wondered, an
example of the bulldog determination that had won England an empire?

Not long after that, Tamara came to me, looking
flustered and desperate. She had to go to California and
had not a rag to wear. Could I possibly help?

I had just returned from shopping in Mexico City
and had bought quite a few clothes. I had gone with a
shrewd shopper and we had found some figured silk
shirts and a wool dressing gown embroidered with gold.

There were a few other things I found to lend to Tamara. She was so grateful, saying over and over how sweet it was of me to lend my clothes to her. She did not know what to do to somehow repay me. That was true enough, for I never again had any of the clothes in my possession, though I caught occasional glimpses of them from time to time.

Lightheartedly, she gave the silk shirt to her sister. She said, "Poor Carola has nothing," and handed it to her — literally the shirt off *my* back. A few days after she returned from California, I dropped in to see her because I happened to be in her neighborhood.

She was wearing the pale wool dressing gown and was in the process of giving a party for all the children in the block. She performed a gay, graceful, pirouette to flare out the robe and said, "Thank you so much for lending me this. I'm just going to have it cleaned and sent over to you."

She never did. I never cared. Tamara was a bright, elusive spirit and it was little enough to pay for her silvery presence.

Taxco was a gentler, more peaceful town than most in Mexico at that time, but there was also a darker side that was occasionally revealed to me. I recall one girl who came weeping to the house to tell her troubles to me. She was the daughter of Herminio Pavan, a little laborer who spent all his earnings on drinking. His problem-plagued wife had finally been forced to take in a boarder in order to eke out a scant living. The boarder slept on the floor of the main room, rolled in a serape. The night before the daughter came to see me, Herminio had come home drunk and had seen the man sleeping on the floor. In an instant fury of jealousy he had pulled out a knife and had plunged it into the sleeping man's heart. His befuddled mind had forgotten about the boarder they had been forced to take in.

Now the girl and her mother would suffer more without the presence of even a drunken breadwinner in the house. There were not enough cooking and housekeeping jobs in Taxco to match the number of women who had to make their own way without husbands to support them. I wanted to do something to help them, but it was not for some time that I found the way.

Another Sunday morning, I had just returned from a walk in the mountains when a girl came running up the hill screaming, "I've been robbed."

At first I could not understand her, for she was shrieking at the top of her voice. Then she threw herself on me and wept hysterically. I could not make any sense out of what she was saying. Then a man I had never seen before came along. He was wielding a big, ugly stick and was about to beat the girl.

"Don't you dare touch her!" I snapped. "You leave her alone." Then I realized I was talking to him in English, so I mustered the little Spanish I knew and said, *"Es una amiga de mía"* — She's a friend of mine.

The stranger glowered at me but did not dare beat the girl while I had my arms around her. She was shaking with terror. The man stood there for a while, trying to think of some way to release his fury. Finally he muttered a curse, threw down the stick and stomped away. By that time I was shaking as much as the girl.

There were so many young girls in Taxco who needed some kind of work and protection from casual predators and in me they seemed to find a sympathetic ear. For a long time I could offer them only advice.

Then Bill approached me one day and announced, "I just built an apartment for you at my place — on the north side, overlooking the barranca."

"That was nice of you," I said, taken aback by the news. "But wouldn't it hurt Natalie's feelings if I moved out of her house?"

"That's no way for you to live," Bill said firmly. "All those parties day and night. You're not that kind."

The continual parties were beginning to pall. I preferred quiet and could only find a pale semblance of it by retreating to my bedroom in Natalie's house.

I looked at the apartment that Bill had built. It was set among begonias and *guayaba* trees and was separated from the main part of the house, with a private entrance. Natalie's earlier suggestion of scandal — "What will people say?" — no longer affected me at all. People could say what they cared to. In Bill's house I would have far more privacy than in Natalie's party-plagued palace.

Telling her this, however, posed a delicate problem of tact. The two houses faced each other across the barranca. Natalie was the "hostess" of Taxco and Bill, in his own way, was the "host." It almost seemed as if I were moving from one camp into an enemy camp. Changing sides.

A frontal assault seemed the best way. I went into Natalie's house on a high note of enthusiasm.

"The most marvelous thing has happened!" I exclaimed.

Natalie looked surprised. "What on earth is it?"

"Well, you know how people are always dropping in on their way to Acapulco?"

"Yes, certainly."

"And they never have the right clothes for the beach and are always borrowing something from us?"

"It's getting so I can't keep any clothes at all around here," Natalie agreed.

237

"Well, from now on, I'm going to sell to them. I'm going to make some clothes myself and have a little shop."

"Do you know anything about making clothes?" Natalie asked dubiously. It was the kind of thing she never dreamed of doing herself.

"Certainly I do. Didn't I tell you I used to make all my own clothes?"

"I guess you did tell me something about that," Natalie said. I pressed closer to the primary point.

"And you know there are dozens of girls in Taxco who do perfectly marvelous embroidery. I've been trying to think of some way to help some of the poor girls in town here."

"I know you have, dear. I have too, but . . ." I could tell that Natalie was picturing her house being invaded by hordes of seamstresses.

"And Bill Spratling has built the most wonderful apartment in the back of his place. If faces the barranca so it overlooks your house. I can do all the sewing there and have the girls come there too."

Natalie relaxed visibly. "I think that's a lovely idea," she said, with the first enthusiasm she had shown. She threw herself into the plans headlong. "But you can't have your shop in Bill's place. It's too high up for most of the tourists to climb. We can find a little place down on the plaza. That'll be easy enough to do. I'll ask around and see what's vacant." She paused. "Oh dear, I will miss you."

"Of course you won't. I'll be right across the barranca. You could throw stones at me."

Natalie laughed. Then, like a general, she began commandeering troops of local boys to carry my possessions across the ravine. It was accomplished in no time at all.

That night I had dinner with Bill and told him how I had managed to persuade Natalie that I was not abandoning her.

Bill nodded thoughtfully. "You'll have to make some kind of token effort at having a shop, I suppose."

"Token indeed! I meant every word I said. You should see some of the embroidery that the women here can do. There was some kind of convent years and years ago but the government closed it down during the Revolution. The nuns taught embroidery to all the girls who went there and it's been passed along from mother to daughter."

Bill liked the idea as he turned it over in his head. "It'd be the same sort of thing I'm doing with silver working," he mused.

239

"Well, no, not on the same scale. But these girls do need organization and some direction. They always like combinations such as lavender and organdy."

It was 1938. The impending war in Europe had begun to stifle the flow of imports from Europe to the United States and the buyers were casting around for another source. They discovered Mexico and Spratling silver which had an elegance that compared favorably with the best of European jewelry. Apart from his designs, Bill's artistry lay in knowing what kind of stones would go well with his silver. Precious stones, such as diamonds or rubies, would diminish the effect of the silver, so Bill used semiprecious stones indigenous to Mexico to enhance his silver rather than to dominate it.

Taxco was becoming a tourist attraction rather than a mere way station on the road to Acapulco. Spratling silver was being sold in the best stores all over the United States. His business in Taxco flourished and many of his workers left to open shops of their own. The best of them was Tony Castillo, who remained a close friend of Bill's all his life.

Almost from the start, the clothing shop I opened was a success. Word had passed swiftly along the magical grapevine of Taxco that I was going to hire expert seamstresses and buy embroidery work. Within days I had seen samples of all the work done in Taxco and had chosen the most skillful girls. I was amazed at how quickly they could master the most intricate embroidery stitches. I would demonstrate an Italian trapunto stitch and they would say, "Oh, we can do that." And they did. The girls sat around in a small room of the apartment, talking and gossiping as they sewed. It amazed the rest of the town to see that women could actually earn money at something other than housework.

Bill worked in his silver factory in the morning and we would meet for lunch at precisely one o'clock. We exchanged the news of the day and compared the male silversmith gossip with the female seamstress gossip and the disparity was astounding. Then we would go our separate ways. In the evenings I went to bed early, while Bill often had a small party with a group of men who played poker and had uproarious good times. The dirtiest of jokes were traded back and forth.

I had often argued with Bill about the merit of a dirty joke. I could not see the point unless the joke had wit as well. But Bill liked them all, and collected them like rare bottles or stamps. At one time I brought a young lady to meet him. She had been wanting to know Bill for some time but had been scared off by his reputation for being irascible — which was only half earned. The young lady liked Bill very much, and to ingratiate herself with him told an incredibly obscene joke. Bill

241

laughed heartily. But the next time I saw him, he said, "Why, that girl — that's the dirtiest story I ever heard."

"Well, didn't you like it?" I asked tartly.

He grinned and said, "It's a good story. Just the wrong mouth for it, I guess."

Margaret Sanger came to Taxco and rented a large, comfortable house. She was in Mexico to look into the birth control situation, but had been unable to accomplish anything because of the church. But in Taxco, she rested and gave a series of parties. Roland Peters, the actor, was a great friend of hers and she and Roland planned a large party to which they invited Bill and me and just about everybody else in Taxco. It was to be held in the Bar Paco, and on the appointed day all the sandwiches were made, the glasses polished, the ice cubes frozen, and the liquor ready.

That same day, Bill said to me, "I'm having a party tonight at the Bar Paco. You'd better come and help make sandwiches or something."

I said, "But Margaret Sanger is having a party tonight."

"Yes," he said, "I invited her and that Peters fellow too."

I was annoyed. Bill rarely went to parties that he did not give himself and this time he had twisted things around so that he *was* giving it himself.

"You idiot!" I exclaimed. "You've misunderstood everything. Don't you know that you were invited to Margaret Sanger's party before you decided to give one of your own? And at the same place, too."

"Is that what happened?" he asked, genuinely puzzled.

I knew it was not malice in Bill, but absentmindedness. Quite often he invited a number of people to lunch at one-thirty. That day he would eat lunch as usual at one o'clock and be truly surprised when his guests trooped in, ready to be feted.

"Yes," I told him, with an air of resignation, "that's what happened."

"Well then, I'll have to cancel my party and go to hers," he said, and laughed.

Bill and I were very good for each other. He always seemed to be like a younger brother or a favorite nephew to me, and we could tell each other anything at all. We treated each other's eccentricities with affectionate respect.

Even when Bill insisted that he was in complete accord with Franco's regime in Spain, we had no difficulties. I argued with him at great length, as did many others, and it always seemed to me that he used his point of contention as the basis for a good, healthy, cathartic argument. A great many Spanish refugees were fleeing to Mexico, among them a number of children whose families had been killed. Bill and I were on the point of adopting one of the children. We were completely charmed by him, even when he resolutely insisted, "I am a Fascist and I'm going to be one for the rest of my life."

Fortunately, I came to my senses in time and said, "This is silly. What do I know about bringing up a child, and for that matter, what do you know about it either?" Sanity prevailed and we allowed the boy to be adopted into a more conventional family.

It was only natural that Bill would expect me to like all his friends. He expected that of people. If he liked someone, then all the other people he liked would have to share his feelings.

It did not always work out that way. Diego Rivera was a close friend of Bill's and he came to Taxco often. After my first encounter with him I tried, discreetly, to avoid him.

Bill and I had gone to Mexico City, and he took me to see Rivera without telling me anything at all about the man. We went to his house and waited for him to appear. Finally, he came down the wrought-iron winding stairs with a monkey in his hand and I thought I had never seen anything so ridiculous. He was a great, gross man cradling a tiny monkey. He brushed aside Bill's introduction of me and immediately began talking about something I could not even understand. At the time, Bill was arranging for the U.S. ambassador, Dwight Morrow, to commission Rivera to do a huge mural in Cuernavaca.

Rivera talked in grandiose terms, gesticulating dramatically as he strode about the room. I stared at him, somewhat repelled and somewhat fascinated. Suddenly I realized what it was in him that had struck a familiar, painful chord.

He reminded me of Sherwood. He had the same absolute involvement in himself, the same lack of awareness of the rest of the world. He loved nothing but his art and cared for only those who could help him achieve it. Later I learned that he was like Sherwood in other ways as well. He had married four wives in a rhythmic cycle of seven years each.

I had not thought of Sherwood in years, ever since I had determined to rid my mind of him. My life had been far too full, and I had no desire to open up old scars. I simply avoided Rivera and never said why.

A girl I knew at Stanford came to Taxco to see me, Mary Anita Loos, the niece of the writer I had known in New Orleans and New York. My apartment was too small to comfortably accommodate her, so she went to live with Rosa and Miguel Covarrubias. Bill Spratling was immediately taken with Mary Anita. They went everywhere together and it seemed to all of Taxco that a great, heady affair was developing between them.

At first I thought it was wonderful that two people I was so fond of might pair off together. I could keep track of them both better. Then I realized it was not wonderful at all. It could never happen. Bill was not the kind of man who could settle into married life. He was not oriented that way. Girls that came to Taxco would fall for him in droves. He had a dynamic, almost mesmerizing personality and knew so much about so many things that girls could not resist him. One young girl fell madly in love with him, or thought she had. She came to see me and said, "You know that man. What am I ever going to do about it? Is it hopeless?"

"My dear," I said, "it's completely hopeless. You can't do a thing. Girls fall for him all the time. Some of them kill themselves on railroad tracks and some of them drown themselves, but there's just nothing to do about it."

She took me perfectly seriously. "Do you really mean that?"

I laughed, but in a way, I really did mean that.

Now it was clear to me that Mary Anita was moving in the same direction and I knew that she would be hurt. Bill was telling everyone that she was his little "*novia,*" which can mean either sweetheart or fiancée. To him, it

246

was a way of expressing his fondness for her. To her it may have meant something more.

Finally I thought, "Heavens, this is never going to come through. Mary Anita is just too young to know what she's doing. It's up to me to do something."

I said to her, "Mary, this isn't the way to behave. If you're not really Bill's *novia*, you shouldn't let him tell people you are."

"Bill would never do anything to hurt me. You know that," she said.

"Of course he wouldn't," I told her, feeling helpless. "But you're the one who has to look out for yourself."

Finally, at dinner one night, something was said to bring up the subject of marriage and whether it would happen between Bill and Mary Anita. It produced an unnerving silence. Then Bill asked if I would leave him alone with Mary Anita. "We'll talk this out," he said, very quietly and gravely.

I was glad that the situation would be resolved, but I knew it would hurt Bill and Anita in the process. Bill apparently told Mary Anita that marriage was not for him and why it was not, for she went back to the Covarrubias house early that night.

All night, people buzzed with speculations and wild guesses, recriminations and defenses. At first they blamed Bill entirely, then they blamed me. They thought

I wanted Bill to myself and that I was jealous. There had never been anything between Bill and myself but a purely platonic relationship. Anything more was unthinkable. Bill and I knew that and so, now, did Mary Anita. After a time the talk died down as talk unnourished by reality will.

Mary Anita went back to California and later married Richard Sale, a novelist. She harbored no bitterness toward Bill, quite the reverse. She returned often to Taxco and Bill and I corresponded with her often.

Bill remained intensely fond of Mary Anita and would often refer to her as "the one great love in my life." But he had carved out an existence for himself in Taxco, a way of life that did not include a wife. It was a rugged male world that no woman could have fitted into. I lived in Bill's house but maintained complete independence from him and our worlds coexisted but did not mingle. When Sherwood left me, I had created for myself a state of mind that did not depend on any other individual. Because of this I made no demands on Bill and he could feel comfortable with me because of that.

 fifteen

From the moment I stepped outdoors one morning I could tell that something had happened. There was a strange, expectant hush in the air, as though all of Taxco had stopped work and was waiting for something. None of the usual sounds of chopping and sawing and pounding could be heard from across the barranca.

Bill would know what was going on. His workers formed a main artery of the grapevine and they would keep him informed. He was still at his breakfast table on the patio when I came up to him. Three of his workers had come up from the factory and were standing around, taking turns chattering to him, and I could not understand a word they said. My Spanish had improved a good deal but it was not up to an excited rush of words. I waited until they were through and Bill had heard everything he thought pertinent.

Finally he dismissed the workers and they moved, still gabbling, toward the front door. "Aha," said Bill. "It's finally happened. Taxco has got itself a first-class scandal."

When he paused, as if to let the suspense build up to the proper pitch, I burst out, "For heaven's sakes, Bill, tell me what it is."

"Some rich gringo from Chicago got chopped up with machetes last night. They found him down in the barranca right underneath your window. Didn't you hear anything last night?"

I sat down, feeling suddenly weak. Bill and I both loved mystery stories, but this was too close to be viewed as an abstract enigma. "I didn't hear a thing," I said.

"No strange noises? Someone thrashing around? *Chopping* noises?" Bill was behaving like Inspector Maigret.

"Not a sound. I was asleep. Now will you please tell me all that you know about this?"

"Well," he began expansively, "a rich American drove into town yesterday in a brand-new Cadillac driven by a chauffeur. He registered at the Hotel Los Arcos and then his chauffeur went to bed and the American went out on the town. Early this morning, José, the carpenter's boy, found him in bloody pieces down in the barranca."

I thought Bill might be stretching the gory potentials of the story, but I said nothing. Bill had his own way of telling a story and it was better than almost anybody else's way.

"And that's not all," Bill said, getting up from the table. "Let's go down to the plaza and take a look at the church."

He refused to say another word about it so I decided to let him play out the story as he pleased. Certainly it was an extraordinary enough event to deserve a buildup. We went out to the Calle de las Delicias and made our way down the narrow lane to the Borda Plaza.

The Santa Prisca church is one of the most impressive sights in Mexico. When it was first built, it was beefsteak red but the climate of Taxco has mellowed it to a quiet pink. Its facade is rococo to an extreme, topped with two towers and two saints. One of the saints is the Virgin and the other is, quite naturally, Santa Prisca. They both stand looking benignly down at the plaza below. Or did.

During the night a strong gale had blown the Virgin off her perch and sent her crashing to the courtyard. We inspected her ruins, then retreated to the Bar Paco for coffee and a different view. The shattered Virgin was surrounded by excited, worried Taxcanians, all of whom were convinced that she had fallen at the exact instant that a machete lopped off the head of the American. God was punishing Taxco for its violence of the night before.

Then a strange phenomenon occurred — something I had never before seen in Taxco. As we sat there looking out at the Plaza, little old ladies swathed in black rebozos came creeping toward the church, limping and inching along from every possible lane and road. They were women that Bill and I had never seen before, so old that they remained in their houses. They had dragged themselves up from their pallets or chairs and had come to pray just as hard as they could to the Virgin, who had clearly thrown herself off the church as a dire portent. If the Virgin were to desert them, what would they have?

Bill thought they looked like little bugs coming out from under a stone and I could not honestly disagree. It was, nevertheless, a solemnly impressive sight.

Despite all the speculative talk that went on in Taxco among the natives and the Americans as well, the mad machete wielder was never found. The U.S. Embassy sent down people to investigate and there was a terrible uproar for a long time but nothing ever came of it.

For some time after that, I viewed Taxco from a different perspective. Did the bland adobe walls conceal seething passions and hatreds?

I stayed too late at Natalie's home one night a few weeks after the machete slaying. Bill had long since gone home and I had no intention of crossing the dark barranca where the killing had taken place. Instead, I went down to the plaza and then started climbing up the street where I lived. There was only a single light bulb in the street and it cast far eerier shadows than any it dispelled. There was not a soul in sight and all the houses were darkened.

Then I came to the four-foot-wide lane that led up to my doorway. It was about fifty yards long and there were cold, blank adobe walls on either side. I stopped dead in my tracks, not even daring to breathe.

Lying halfway across the path was a man, stretched out flat. Was he dead, another victim of the machete killer? His leg twitched and then I thought of the other alternative — having to get by him. "My time has come," I thought. I waited there for an eternity, but I knew I would have to get past the sodden obstacle.

I moved a few tentative steps closer, then paused again. He was moving! Making a great effort, the man was raising his head a few inches off the cobblestone that was his pillow. He looked at me through liquor-bleared eyes and said, *"Pase, Señora."*

Having been given the traditional polite permission to pass, I delicately skirted the man's head as he laid it back down on the cobblestone, and I moved on down the lane, shaking with suppressed laughter.

In my eyes, Taxco had returned to its normal peacefulness, even though there were a few isolated incidents that threw the town into a chattering tizzy. None of them ever brought the little old ladies out to pray and that, I think is the true gauge of a disaster in Taxco.

Pedro Parmelo was a very smart bookkeeper who knew all the tricks and could untangle the complexities of the tax laws. He kept my books as well as Bill's and was very highly regarded in Taxco. He kept his finger firmly planted on the financial pulse of the town and knew to the penny what everybody made and how they made it.

Pedro also owned a newspaper that was printed in Iguala, a tiny town about sixteen miles from Taxco. He hired men from both Taxco and Iguala to work for him, but he had a bad habit of paying the men only when the newspaper happened to be profitable enough for him to easily afford the wages.

One of the men who worked for Pedro was a schoolteacher, and he was particularly upset about not having been paid the way he should have been. He went to see Pedro one dark night in a effort to get his money.

The night, however, proved to be too dark for the schoolteacher's good, for Pedro Parmelo later testified that he had seen a strange man trying to climb up his walls and get into his house. Protecting home and family, Pedro whipped out a pistol and shot at the intruder. He had only meant to scare the man away, but Pedro was a bad shot and the bullet struck the schoolteacher in the heart.

There was a fine, elaborate funeral for the schoolteacher, attended by all the schoolchildren and all the sympathetic underpaid workers in Taxco. It was a major turnout.

Pedro Parmelo was unable to attend, for he had been placed in jail. Undaunted, he continued with his business just the same. He borrowed a table and a chair from me and went on keeping books for all of Taxco. He hired a man to carry the books back and forth from the jail to his varied clientele. Much later, when there was to be a trial, he was taken to Mexico City. I never learned what his sentence was, but evidently it was suspended, because he went on being a successful bookkeeper in Mexico City and did a thriving business.

Our next bookkeeper was a great fat lumbering

creature named Corteo. Every time I saw him he would pat me on the back in a very friendly way and call me by some other name. "Señora Margarita," he would say, "you don't know how delighted I am to see you."

Corteo took over Pedro Parmelo's bookkeeping, and after a number of months, Bill and several other silversmiths went to see him about a curiosity they had discovered in their books. Taxes in Mexico are supposed to be paid every month, but upon examination of all the books they found that they had not been paid for at least three months.

"What is going on here, Señor Corteo?" he was asked.

He shrugged and waved his hand expansively. "Oh, I'm going to pay that. I need the money to finish building my house. I'll have it back in the bank in no time."

Well, Taxco is a relaxed town, so Bill and the others took Corteo's word for it and let him juggle the books as he pleased. But Bill was doing a great deal of business in those wartime days and the government somehow got word of the crafty machinations of Señor Corteo. A tax man came down to look into the matter and to talk it over with Corteo, who was, after all, the government's representative in Taxco.

They talked and talked, but Corteo simply did not think he had done anything wrong. He had only used the money for a little while, and only because he had wanted to finish the house and provide a roof over the heads of his beloved family. The Mexican government could surely understand that.

The tax man from Mexico City was reasonable, but he did think Corteo was making too much money one way and another. He finally said that the government would remove Corteo from his post in Taxco and assign him to a much smaller town where he would make a much smaller amount of money. Perhaps Cuautla.

At this point Señor Corteo raised his hand politely. "No," he said. "I am resigning."

That settled the issue to everyone's satisfaction and a new tax man was assigned to Taxco. Corteo went into business for himself and flourished as never before.

The only way that World War II affected Taxco was in the great increase in business. Buyers were desperate for luxury goods to sell in the United States. They came down to Taxco and found a wealth of things such as baskets, rebozos, pottery and serapes. Enthusiastically they decided that such items would sell wonderfully in better stores and offered to buy all that the local craftsmen could turn out. "Fine," thought the craftsmen. "We'll make twenty a week instead of only one." What no one had anticipated was that the quality of the work would be drastically lowered. When the buyers returned, they decided that they no longer wanted the goods and all the hopes of financial salvation in Taxco were destroyed. Bill turned out a great deal of jewelry in those days but was too canny to lower the quality of his goods. It is impossible to mass-produce hand embroidery, so my business prospered, but not beyond its reasonable limits.

After Pearl Harbor, Mexico came into the war on the side of the United States, of course, and for a while I was worried that Bill might be seized with a fit of patriotism and try to join the army. He was forty-one at the time, however, so my fears were groundless.

There were a few Germans living in Taxco and they had to go to Mexico City each month to report. It was mostly just a nuisance for them, for they could hardly have engaged in much subversive espionage in Taxco. One of them came into my shop, leaned his elbow on the counter, and said, "Don't worry. You've always been nice to me and my wife. We'll look out for you when the war is over."

Bill's closest friend in Mexico was Miguel Covarrubias. They swapped pre-Columbian pieces together and went off on many trips to find new ones. Miguel was a handsome man, sweet-tempered and gentle, and he was married to a woman who was not at all like him in temperament or style. Rosa Covarrubias was a vivacious and flashing woman who seemed the least likely match for the quiet Miguel. She had been a dancer even though she was more voluptuous than most dancers. Her fiery-tempered spats with Miguel were exhausting for both of them, and when she came to Taxco to rest, she decided to help out with my budding clothing shop.

Rosa had a great many friends, both famous and rich, and in no time they were all coming to the shop. Rosa would stay in Taxco for a few weeks and then go off on trips to various places. She was an unpredictable and erratic partner, but fun when she was around and she did bring many customers into the store. The problem was that we would make plans together about the kind and quantity of the clothes we would turn out and then Rosa would find it necessary to vanish for weeks at a time. I would be left with more work than I could manage.

We were in the shop together one day, working on some new design, and the man she was going with then was sitting around watching and chatting. Rosa suddenly threw her hands up in the air and moaned, "Oh, you cut this out. I just don't know how to do it."

Her friend broke in indignantly. "You cut it out yourself. You always give Elizabeth all the hard work to do."

Rosa reacted as though I had made the remark myself, for she launched into a long tirade and finally ended by saying that she had too many social obligations in Mexico City that she could no longer neglect. I would just have to run the clothing shop without her.

I was very fond of her and sorry to see her go, but I knew that I would be better off if I did my own planning to suit my own capacities. We severed business, but not social, relations.

My idea, in starting the dress shop, was to sell clothes that would be suitable for Acapulco and have a distinctly Mexican touch. One of the first products was a pink blouse with very small checks and a skirt made from a blue and white striped rebozo. Rosa took the dress to New York to an elegant dress salon which agreed to sell as many as we could turn out.

Rosa told all the famous people she knew about the dress shop in Taxco and the word was spread around that this was the place to go en route to Acapulco. I got to know a surprising number of celebrities simply by staying in the shop.

One Sunday morning a girl who worked for me showed up at my apartment with a sad tale about how she needed a certain sum of money immediately for her ailing parents. As her story grew in complexity it waned in credibility, and I was sure the girl wanted money for a new dress or a present for an errant *novio*. I usually found it prudent to go along with this kind of plea for money because by the time the girl had worked herself into the proper pitch of passion for the recital, she half believed it herself and would have considered it a breach of faith had I refused her. She would have been shocked and offended that I could have so little concern for the welfare of her family.

Sunday morning, however, is a bad time for such requests, for it is impossible to cash a check through normal channels. I went over to Bill's house to ask if he had any money. He had a visitor so I waited outside the patio until he could break away from his conversation to see me. Then I told him what I wanted.

Loudly, Bill said, "Come on inside. There's a fellow in here who's got all the money in the world. He can cash your check for you if anybody can — maybe even give you a grant."

It was the first time I met Nelson Rockefeller and I was a little embarrassed — particularly when it turned out that he did not, in fact, have enough cash on him to cover the check. Bill thought that was hilarious and after a while so did Nelson. Finally Bill dug up the money and I gave it to the girl with the erstwhile ailing parents.

Cary Grant came to Taxco while he was married to Barbara Hutton, and a curious competition developed between them. Barbara designed a ring and Bill Spratling was deft enough to make her ring look good when he made the ring for her. She presented it to Cary Grant, who immediately bought something for her from Bill's shop that cost even more than the ring. Then Barbara began glancing around to find something even more expensive and Cary did the same. It would have been marvelous for Bill's business had it gone on long enough. But Barbara was having a siege of being afraid she would be kidnapped at that time, and perhaps she decided that the flaunting of too much silver might make her an even more tempting target. At any rate, the competition halted and the bodyguard who followed them about wearing a shoulder holster and an enormous gun did not even have the grace to look relieved.

One of the movie companies in Hollywood had gotten into trouble by not paying a certain tax. They absolved themselves by blaming a scapegoat, who promptly ran off to Mexico and stayed at the Hotel Los Arcos in Taxco. Paulette Goddard came to visit him from time to time for he did not dare go back to the United States. Paulette was a bold and saucy girl with mischief in her eyes and sparkle in her smile. She bought a number of things from me and ordered several more. We got along very well, though I thought her romance with the Hollywood exile could have been more discreetly managed.

I decided it would be amusingly appropriate to embroider in Spanish an old Mexican adage along the hem of the skirt she had ordered. She was delighted with the embroidery and wore the skirt everywhere, completely mystified at the hilarious reaction it evoked in those who could read Spanish. Paulette, of course, had no idea what the translation was, but finally someone told her: "If you want to get on in this world, walk alone. He who leans gets bent." She laughed, perhaps a bit uneasily, and avoided buying embroidery in the form of words or phrases from then on.

Lauren Bacall, a tall handsome girl with the cool gray eyes of an aristocrat, went stalking about the shop one day, haughty and aloof as a Russian wolfhound. I began to be annoyed at her somewhat disdainful reaction to the dresses I had made so carefully, and with my annoyance, my own hauteur expanded. Finally we were both stiff as sticks, and as friendly.

Humphrey Bogart had been sitting at one side of the shop, watching the show. He said to me, "Don't mind her — she doesn't know anything about manners anyway."

It was as if Humphrey had flicked a switch in Betty Bacall, for immediately she became warm and friendly to me. It was such a surprise that it took a moment for my own haughty pose to dissipate, but then we chatted amicably and in time we became good friends. She had been cast as a rather simpleminded, frivolous girl in a movie called *How to Marry a Millionaire,* and wanted to find the clothes to fit the role. I made her a half dozen frothy, pretty dresses which made quite a hit, she told me later.

Helena Rubenstein visited Bill Spratling at his newly acquired house in Acapulco and Bill asked me to come down and meet her. In those days, Acapulco was not the plastic parody of paradise it is today. It was lively and popular with tourists, but it was still a place where one could relax quietly with friends.

Helena Rubenstein was a fascinating creature, short, with the stocky silhouette of a Russian peasant. Her black, active eyes searched and probed like surgical instruments. Wherever she went she was accompanied by her husband, the Georgian prince who was never referred to, or known as, anything but the Prince, while I knew him.

We spent a peaceful evening on the beach watching the long, luminescent rollers gliding up to the shore and breaking in a crystalline spray. Helena Rubenstein kept us entertained with stories about her enormous business that she had built up from nothing. At one point she had grown tired of running it and had sold it for an astronomical price. But without her aggressive drive, the business soon faltered and lagged. Unwilling to see the monument she had constructed collapse, she finally bought it back for half the money she had paid for it. It had been a most profitable exchange.

In the morning, Bill and I were having breakfast out on the patio when Helena and the Prince came out to join us. She was wearing what, on any normal human being, would have been a string of beads. Admiring them, I said, "What a pretty color!"

She looked at me sharply for a moment, then said flatly, "They ought to be a pretty color. They're pigeon egg rubies."

I went back to eating breakfast without a word for there was nothing I could say to that. Later that day we all went back to Taxco, where Valentin Vidaretta had arranged to give a party for Helena and the Prince in the huge old Hacienda del San Juan de Batista. Everyone in town had been invited and we had pooled our servants to create a great and lavish *olla* of potted pigeons.

The servants had been all over town, snaring and netting the pigeons, which were cleaned, plucked and plunked into a vast caldron. The ancient hacienda had been cleaned to perfection and the Olympic-size swimming pool with its Romanesque arches had been scrubbed down.

When everyone was assembled, the pigeons were served with high ceremony. The pigeons were a better idea than accomplishment, it seemed to me, for there was very little substance to them. I watched the people around me delicately carving away at the breasts, which held the only meat on the pigeons. Then I saw Valentin staring as if hypnotized at Helena Rubenstein. She was seated in the place for the guest of honor, of course, and was eating with truly remarkable gusto. She picked up a pigeon in her hands and proceeded to methodically devour it — breast, legs, neck, and bones. She returned not a trace of the bird to her plate. Valentin visibly shook himself out of his trance and, excellent host that he was, followed suit, doggedly wolfing the entire bird.

Helena was a great hit with everyone at the party. Her brusque, pithy pronouncements dazzled them and were simple to translate into Spanish.

The next day, she came poking and picking around in my shop, looking for something she might care to buy. The Prince picked up a light gray woolen shawl with a green pattern and a marvelous texture and said, "Now this takes my eye. Why don't you buy it?"

She peered closely at the shawl and then put it down decisively. "No. I don't want it. It's no good."

I said: "Why, I thought it was very nice."

She picked it up again and looked at it even more closely, fingering the material. Then she said, "Well, it's nice enough," and put it back down again. Nothing more was said about the shawl. Instead, she spotted some paintings that I had bought, little portraits of children in the colonial days of Mexico.

She began stacking up the paintings, muttering that she would take them along with her. I had one of my girls package them and they went off to the United States with Helena and the Prince. I remarked casually to Bill that it was curious that no mention had been made of paying for the paintings.

"Oh that's just her way," he said. "She never carries any money with her. She'll send you a check."

Instead, she sent a brief note to the effect that the paintings were fakes and were being returned. I wondered what rare old masters she thought she had uncovered. I had bought them simply as delightful portraits and was just as pleased to have them back.

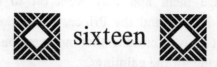 sixteen

When I had first come to Mexico, Bill Spratling held a celebration of the anniversary of his silver factory, which he called Las Delicias, after the street on which he lived. Each year after that, Bill's workers held a party that grew in enthusiasm and scope. When some of the more talented workers opened shops of their own, they still met with Bill each year for the anniversary party.

Then the State of Guerrero officially declared it a state holiday, "The Day of Silver in Taxco," and prizes were awarded to the best silverwork done each year. Famous people flew in from all over the world to attend and the judging was done by such distinguished artists as Rufino Tamayo and José Clemente Orozco. The holiday was stretched out to become Silver Week. Finally the national government stepped in and placed the entire fiesta in the hands of a nonprofit civic foundation. The prizes for the silverwork were greatly increased and all of Mexico was invited to enter into the competition.

I had been present at the first anniversary party of Las Delicias, with only a few workers and Bill unceremoniously toasting a single slim year of existence. From a mere pause in the day's work, it had mushroomed into a national celebration and it was a rare, curious experience to witness the entire process.

By the end of the war, Bill had over four hundred silversmiths working for him and had expanded into the Hacienda del Florida, outside Taxco. The silver industry had contracted the common disease of "gigantism" and could not but suffer for it. Bill's sudden, sweeping expansion forced him to look for outside money to finance it, and the outside money appeared in the form of an American who promptly proceeded to run the industry into the ground by taking over the management from Bill.

It was not, then, a rare occurrence for a sharp financier in the United States to take over a company with an eye to quick profits and an overall loss of money for tax purposes. This kind of maneuver always results in hardships and misfortunes. But in Taxco, the financier was tampering with the very life of an entire town and industry.

It also put an end to Bill's silver factory in Taxco. He resigned from the tottering corporate structure of Las Delicias, which had been renamed Spratling y Artesanos, and moved to a small ranch at Taxco-el-Viejo, about two thousand feet lower in altitude than Taxco.

Bill had acquired the ranch some years before. During the war, we had been thinking of buying a ranch up in the hills and had found one we liked. He gave the owner a hundred pesos down on the property and agreed to wait until the corn harvest was in before the negotiations would go any farther. We waited until the corn was in, then went out to the ranch. The owner and all his family were out in the field, industriously planting more corn. "You'll have to wait until this corn is in, too," we were told. It began to dawn on us that the man had no intention of selling his property to us.

We began driving around the countryside, looking for some other place. We found a large piece of property halfway between Taxco and Iguala that extended from the highway to the river. Water was an absolute necessity for the ranch that Bill planned, and this one was copiously supplied by the river and a number of springs.

Bill bought it on the spot, for he had plenty of money in those days.

The masons around Taxco seemed to have a natural genius for their trade and Bill was able to have a house built on his ranch in a matter of days. For some reason of his own, he told people he was buying the ranch for me. It seemed to be a private joke between him and his sense of humor. I was never able to understand the point of it.

Bill was so delighted with the house he had designed that he began to live in it part of the time. When he lost most of his money with the collapse of Las Delicias he moved out there to live on practically nothing while he replanned his future.

I remained in Taxco at the house on Las Delicias, and moved into the part of the house that Bill had vacated, using the rest of the place for my seamstresses.

Without Bill's presence, the general quality of the silver that was made in Taxco fell off, for Bill had exerted a strong influence with his designs. He was frankly copied and was a good source of taste and imagination for the other silversmiths. Some of Bill's former workers were very talented and had fresh new ideas of their own. Tony Castillo had devised the idea of wedding various metals together into fine pieces of

271

jewelry and Tony Pineda was also an excellent craftsman. But the town needed Bill's unique flair and missed him badly, though it may not have been generally recognized at the time.

In 1947 Bill opened another workshop at his ranch, and William Spratling, S.A. was a success from the start. He employed only a few silversmiths but they were the best in Taxco and were happy to work for the man who had created the entire industry and had trained all the best silversmiths in Taxco.

Bill kept his business small this time, and continued to do so for the rest of his life. Never again was he tempted to expand or to seek alien capital. Instead, he turned out a select line of exquisite jewelry which made him famous. He continued to contribute to Silver Week in both time and money, and in 1953 Taxco proclaimed him *Hijo Predilecto* — favorite son. They also named a street after him — Calle de Guillermo Spratling.

This final accolade proved to be too much for some of the pettier spirits in Taxco. They had all been greatly pleased with the annual celebration which brought so much prosperity to Taxco, but now they began an insidious campaign. "They" is a term that cannot be more specifically defined. It encompasses less successful souls who were envious of Bill's fame and flourishing business. "They" began to think, "What's he got to do with running this town? He's an American. Why should people go around calling him the 'Unofficial Mayor of Taxco'? And there's that other American here too, a woman, and she's got all the best seamstresses working for her."

That part of it, at least, was true. I did have the best embroideresses in Taxco. They were old friends of mine and I paid them more than they could have earned elsewhere. They were quite content to be working for an American.

There are, in Mexico, a great many little newspapers called *escandalistas*, which are mostly touted in town plazas all over Mexico. Such newspapers, unlike the *Excelsior* or the *Novedades* of Mexico City, contain little or no news. Instead they are devoted to denouncing various people who presumably did not care to pay to have the article suppressed. Often such papers work against each other in a profitable partnership.

One day a person who did occasional legal work for me showed me a paper with an article in it about an unnamed American woman who was holding, in a form of financial bondage, a number of seamstresses in Taxco. She was, the article stated, monopolizing all the best workers and providing unfair competition for the rest of the town.

The man translated the article for me into clumsy

English and then offered to write an article for the rival *escandalista* in which he would defend me from these libelous charges. I declined. The article had named no one and clearly it could not have referred to me. I held no one in bondage of any kind and had absolutely no reason to want myself defended.

The man persisted. It would cost me only three hundred pesos, he said, halving his original offer. I declined again, this time emphatically, and later learned he had written the libelous piece himself.

When the papers turned, like snarling wolves, on Bill Spratling, they printed monstrous attacks on his work, his personal life, and his integrity. One such attack was boldly headlined, "Spratling Is a Thief," and accused him of smuggling pre-Columbian treasures out of Mexico. Another article accused him of seducing the male youth of Taxco.

Bill had invested his very life in Taxco and he was bitterly hurt by the assaults, though he knew they were not believed nor condoned by any of the decent people of the town and his many friends in Taxco assured him of this.

He never went into Taxco again as long as he lived, except after dark to visit a few friends. When he came to see me, he would have to climb the short, steep street named Calle de Guillermo Spratling. It must have been a bitter experience for him. From my balcony he could look out at the many houses he had designed and built in part or in whole.

If anyone wanted to see Bill Spratling, they would have to take the fifteen-minute drive to Taxco-el-Viejo. And a great many people did travel out to the ranch. Every tourist who entered Taxco was driven out there by eager cab drivers or taken by tourist guides, who received a percentage of what was bought. He lost none of his business, as his ranch became a highlight of tours.

Bill soon recovered from his bitterness, for it was hardly an unpleasant self-imposed exile. It was actually much better for him to live at the ranch — he could create his own life and shape his own surroundings. He had planned the house and planted the greenery around it. Like a piece of his silver, it was a Spratling design, to please himself and no other.

On casual inspection, the jungle around the house appeared wild and disordered — an unplanned profusion of African tulips, mangoes and orange trees, ten kinds of banana trees, guavas, tamarinds, and plants of all kinds. Inside the house, there was an open corridor running along another, smaller patio with more plants and trees, fountains and large pre-Columbian objects, and a small guesthouse.

Bill had a great collection of books given to him by

his friends who wrote them or collected by him according to his fancy. Scattered about the main living room
were treasures of ancient art from Mexico, New Guinea,
Africa and Alaska. The furniture was handcrafted and
heavy, with leather chairs and wooden tables. It was a
male sanctuary and a very fine one, but it never occurred
to me that anyone but Bill could live there.

Then, because of a building project that threatened
to cut right through Las Delicias, I had to think about
moving elsewhere. I looked around and then Bill said,
"Why don't you come out and live here at the ranch with
me? It'd be a good place for you. We always had a good
time together."

The idea was patently absurd and I told him so. The
girls who did embroidery work for me could not possibly
get out to the ranch and back each day, and I would be
cut off from my shop on the plaza. Other than that, the
ranch had been built for a man, and a single one at
that. It could no more accommodate a woman living
there than it could a tribe of pygmies.

But Bill was persistent, even stubborn, when he got
an idea into his head. He was always arranging people's
lives with the very best of intentions, though not always
the best of results. Once he decided that one of his
workers, a boy named Miguel, would be wise to marry a
girl who also worked for him. He set about achieving

that goal by flinging them together at odd moments and by telling everybody on the ranch that they were *novios*.

For some time I thought he would succeed in his Machiavellian love plot. I asked him why he insisted on forcing this match and he said it would be a good thing for the factory. They would be married and it would keep them there.

Finally Miguel braced himself and told Don Guillermo that he just did not love this particular girl. She was very nice, *muy simpática*, but just not his cup of *atole*. He had another girl in Taxco he would rather marry.

Bill was somewhat put out about this, but I pointed out to him that the girl would have had a baby and he would have lost her anyway. That was something he had not thought of and it cheered him considerably. He decided he would let true love take its course.

Now he was determined that I should move out to his ranch and live there. To indicate to him the degree of my own determination, I found a house directly across the street from his old house on Delicias, and I moved into it. It was a fine place, high up in the center of Taxco with a good view of Santa Prisca, but Bill remained unconvinced that I was really set in my decision. "It's too uncomfortable out there," I told him. He said it would be all fixed up for me. "What would I do all day without my work?" I objected. He said he would transport my girls out to the ranch every day. Still I held out.

After months of this, he finally snapped, "Well, I'm not going to ask you again to come out here."

I sighed with exaggerated relief. "That's exactly what I've been asking you not to do for two months," I told him.

He did, however, bring it up in a few months. I cut him off short. "Don't even talk to me about it, because I can't do it and you knew perfectly well you wouldn't like it yourself more than two minutes."

He laughed. "Of course, Elizabeth. You live wherever you want." The siege was over.

Bill established a way of life for himself that did not vary in the slightest detail. Over the years he had determined which hours of the day he was most alert and productive and which hours he was least of both. He set his schedule accordingly and nothing could make him deviate from it.

He arose early, at five-thirty, and worked in the morning, with a long siesta in the afternoon. Promptly at five, an ancient parrot, the sole inhabitant and proprietor of a large mango tree, would yank on a chain which rang the bell to announce the closing time of the factory. This was also the cocktail hour.

Bill often had guests who stayed in the small house that was separated from the main quarters by a jungle-like patio. Their presence never diverted Bill from his appointed routine. He would go off to bed at eight-thirty, telling a guest to stay up and drink as long as he pleased. But after about half an hour, when Bill's light was turned off in his bedroom, the night watchman would turn off the electric generator and the guest would be sitting in a totally dark room with a half-finished glass of scotch in his hand. Some were persistent enough to light a kerosene lamp and continue drinking, but most of them simply gave up and went to bed.

One guest told me that he had gone off to bed when the lights were turned off. Bill had warned him that outside the guest house, a Mexican guard would be patrolling the area with a shotgun and that two Great Danes would be prowling the dark patio.

In the middle of the night, Bill's guest leaped out of bed with a sharp pain shooting through his foot. He hobbled over to the lantern and fumbled with matches until he had lit it. Then he went back to the bed to see what had bitten him — a large, evil-looking scorpion. He smashed the scorpion with a paperback novel he had been reading earlier, and sat down with a glass of straight scotch to think about what he should do. He had always heard that scorpion bites could kill a person or make him drastically ill. He had heard that the light brown scorpions in the lowlands could kill a man but that the darker ones in the hills could not. Or was it the other way around? In Cuernavaca someone had told him the cure was to pack the victim's mouth with salt to draw out the poison and prevent lockjaw.

There was nothing he could do, the guest decided. For the life of him — literally — he could not recall the Spanish word for scorpion and there was no way to tell the guard what the trouble was. He might get shot in the process or be torn apart by slavering Great Danes. He sat there awhile, much aware of the hot throbbing in his foot, then took two tranquilizers and finally went back to bed to lie there rigidly, staring up at the ceiling and waiting to either die or become violently ill.

Nothing happened and finally he went to sleep. In the morning he told Bill what had happened.

"*Alacrán*," Bill told him. "*Alacrán* is the word for scorpion. They're not too poisonous around here."

"I'm glad to hear it."

"And the next time it happens, just don't pay any attention to the guard. The shotgun isn't loaded anyway. Just come to me and I've got a certain medicine that will take care of you."

Next time? the guest wondered. Hastily, he devised

business in Mexico City that made it imperative for him to return that day.

It may have been Bill's subtle way of making room for the next guest to arrive.

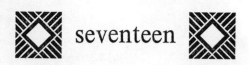 seventeen

It was a bad time in Taxco. Tourist trade had unaccountably fallen off, and what was worse, those tourists who did appear were reluctant to spend their money on local goods. My own business was mostly unaffected, for I had a large roster of customers who wrote me their orders. But the rest of Taxco was languishing in the economic lag.

Painters, particularly, found it hard to peddle their wares. Their art style had not changed; they still whipped out bright and picturesque paintings of "quaint old Taxco" with Santa Prisca dominating the scene and dark green laurel trees splashed about in the middle of the picture. But no one was buying these perennial favorites.

The artists sat about in the Plaza Borda, trading complaints and commiserations.

Only one artist flourished. Miguel Berrio. Miguel strolled about town with his wallet stuffed with pesos and his paintings dwindling steadily, only to be replaced with more. Everyone was mystified by it. Miguel was certainly not the best painter in the town; indeed, many thought he might qualify as the worst. He turned out bright, frothy things with little regard for color, content, or composition. Yet he was selling them when no one else could sell.

What was Miguel's secret? the local artists wondered, and for a time they began to imitate his haphazard, rather amateurish painting style. It did not help them at all and, mercifully, they went back to their own individual styles. Could it be his sales pitch? The way he dressed?

Miguel came often to see me and one day, after having undermined his resistance with cordiality, tea, and pastries, I approached the subject.

"Miguel, how on earth do you manage to sell your paintings? Everyone else is complaining dreadfully."

He hesitated. "You won't tell anyone?" he whispered, though there was not another soul around.

"Miguel, I swear I won't say a word."

He looked around furtively and then leaned closer

rice, and using a steaming tortilla to daintily wipe her fingers.

Then they retired by the flickering, feeble light of a kerosene lamp. The two Americans lay flat on their backs on the cots, staring up at the thatched roof and waiting for some strange, deadly insect to drop down on them. Anna, who had slept quite comfortably on dirt floors in the past, curled up snugly on the cot and went to sleep. She awoke once during the night and saw the two Americans, still staring up at the thatch.

In the morning, the two women begged Anna to take them back to civilization, but there was no bus until late in the afternoon. In the meantime, Anna informed them, she had business in another town down the road. It was even smaller than the one in which they had spent the night. The town was three miles away and Anna set off down the path that led to it, followed closely by the two Americans who did not dare remain behind.

The Indians in the next town had never seen Americans before, nor Germans either, Anna told me. They spoke almost no Spanish but Anna had a smattering of Nahuatl, the ancient tongue of the Aztecs, and she was able to communicate to them her wish to see any hand-woven material that was made in the village. One of the women took Anna off to another part of the village, leaving the two Americans surrounded by a crowd of curious natives. Anna glanced back at her companions. The women in the village were fascinated by them. They fondled them like dolls, running their hands lovingly over the strange materials in the clothes they wore and touching their ashen faces affectionately. The Americans stood paralyzed by fright, not daring to move or to complain.

Anna looked at the materials she was shown, bought some and then went back to rejoin her tour companions. They were seated stiffly on the ground, eating now, and still surrounded by a cluster of admiring women.

Anna dramatically described to me what it was that the two Americans were eating. "It was a tortilla — a huge tortilla! The biggest tortilla I have ever seen in my life — *enormous*! And a piece of dirty, rancid cheese, with big black flies over everything. They were sitting there, choking down little pieces of the food."

Anna rescued the Americans and started them walking back to the first village. She could not resist asking them why they had elected to eat the disgusting food they had been offered — probably as a joke. The Americans looked at her in surprise, and one of them said, "At the Embassy they told us that if we didn't eat the food they gave us, they would *kill* us!"

Anna said she had started to laugh so hard that she nearly fell down, and when she had finally been able to control herself, she carefully explained to the two women that Mexico was not Africa: "Maybe in Africa you must eat the sacred monkey meat or be boiled in a big pot. But in Mexico, if you turn down food, they just give it to someone else."

Anna had many other adventures in her travels, but never again in the company of two such innocents as those. It was faster and simpler to travel alone, and she was quite sure that her traveling companions had confined their subsequent jaunts to organized tours to Diners Club affiliated restaurants and nightclubs only.

On a number of occasions, wealthy Americans have come to settle down in Taxco, and sometimes they fall in love and marry native Taxcanians. When this happens, the wealthy American usually dies first, since they have married someone much younger than themselves. Thus, a class of nouveaux riches is created, and the money is spent in curious ways. One man who had been newly ennobled by the riches of an ancient crone unexpectedly took up religion. He began to bombard the church of Santa Prisca with gifts, not all of which were entirely welcome, for he lacked in taste what he had in fervor. Without consulting the church officials, he had the statue of St. Anthony gilded so that it dazzled the eye and dominated all else. For a time he was muttering about restoring the exterior of the church to its original beefsteak red, but the priests intervened. Thwarted, he cast his eye about the church's interior for another project.

The saints looked too old-fashioned for him, particularly the female saints. Women did not look like that any more — sexless and slim as boys. He decided to bring them ever so slightly up to date. All the saints wore robes of richly embroidered velvet and satin and he began gradually to add stuffing. Pleased with the immediate results, he decided that if a little was good, a lot would be wonderful.

It blossomed into a major scandal in Taxco. The church was the laughingstock of tourists and the townswomen emerged from the church blushing. Yet it was hardly something one could discuss with the priests.

I became so intrigued by the gossip that I went to Santa Prisca to see for myself. The man who had married neither wisely nor well had ingeniously padded all the female saints so that their contours would not have been out of place in a beauty parade. To a saint, they were flaunting great, billowing bosoms, and the priests were for a time ignoring the matter, for they were not willing to risk offending the source of considerable largesse. Finally someone quietly removed all the padding, probably at night, and the sanctity of Santa Prisca was restored.

Others of the nouveau riche ilk used their money to build prestige. One woman whose wealthy husband had died years before spent her widowhood in meeting people who were famous. Whenever anyone who was important in any way came to Taxco, the widow would hold a party for him.

There was a new young man in town. His parents had been persuaded that he was a genius and had given him enough money to spend a year in Taxco writing his masterpiece. He could neither spell nor paragraph and the material he read to me was impossibly dull, but he kept at it persistently. Finally I gently refused to hear any more of it for fear that I might be forced to tell him what I thought of it. He was a nice boy, but at an age where he was still growing up and was particularly awkward at it. I got along well with him once I had eliminated his literary endeavors from our acquaintance-ship.

One day he met Thornton Wilder in the plaza and brought him to meet me. It was four o'clock and they had been invited to the widow's inevitable cocktail party at five. Mr. Wilder and I had a pleasant conversation about the old days. He had known Sherwood and we had a great many other mutual friends. He was a courtly and gallant man.

At five, they went off to the cocktail party and I went back to my own work. Later in the evening, the young man came running down the hill to see me. He was breathless and giggling so hard he was completely unable to speak. I waited and listened to him giggle, until the spasm had subsided. Finally he told me about the widow's cocktail party.

"Everyone was all dressed up and the widow had on her best 'grande dame' manners," he burbled. "Everything was just too elegant for words. When we got there, they were all sitting around as if they were waiting for the second coming! Then the widow swooped over to us and led us around to introduce us to every single person in that place."

At this point he went off into another wild peal of laughter. I waited.

"But you know what?" he exploded. "She kept on introducing Thornton Wilder as 'that famous engineer who built all those bridges in South America.' " The boy collapsed into hilarity and this time I joined in the fun. The widow had obviously heard something about the Bridge of San Luis Rey and Thornton Wilder and had made the connection in her own inimitable way.

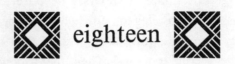

eighteen

Every Monday morning, Bill Spratling would bound out of bed at five o'clock, eat a hasty breakfast and rush out to his car to drive up to Mexico City, about three hours away. He always told me he had to go to the city once a week in order to save money on his telephone bill, but that was a polite fiction.

The idea of Bill economizing on telephoning was patently absurd. He telephoned people constantly, with no thought to the astronomical bill he received monthly. If he had no guest staying with him and he felt like talking, he would call someone he knew in New York or New Orleans and chat for an hour. If he happened to be having a discussion of modern art, he might call Rene d'Harnoncourt in New York to settle an issue; if he were talking about movies, he would call John Huston, whether he were in Ireland or Africa. The telephone was as necessary to Bill as food.

His weekly drive to Mexico City was his own personal Grand Prix.

Bill's chauffeur would be waiting for him at a gas station in Iguala — he never took the other route that led through Taxco. The chauffeur would climb into the back seat and go to sleep after synchronizing his watch with Bill's, and carefully writing down the time of departure. Then Bill would take off on his weekly race with his chauffeur. Bill drove to Mexico City just as fast as he could and the chauffeur would drive back and try to beat Bill's time, which he was rarely able to do.

Bill had a new Mustang which he was proud of and would roar around curves and up mountainsides at speeds which frightened me even to hear about. I rarely slept well on Sunday nights, thinking about Bill's race in the early hours of the morning.

He generally arrived in Mexico City around eight o'clock and would go to a Turkish bath for a thorough steaming and a rubdown to keep himself fit. He had been going to the same Turkish bath for years and knew all the attendants well. When one of them invited him to a fiesta being held for his saint's day Bill was as pleased as if he had been asked to a state dinner at the President's house. He went to the fiesta and enjoyed himself hugely.

Scrubbed pink and feeling refreshed, Bill would head for the bar at the Monte Cassino Hotel where a table was always set aside for him. Here he would hold court and dozens of people would drop by to talk or to trade pre-Columbians with him. Bill's lunchtime drink at his ranch was always a dry martini but for some reason he had whiskey sours at the Monte Cassino. For Bill, a drink was a ceremony and its details were to be fastidiously observed.

At precisely one o'clock, Bill would go over to the Bellenhauser Restaurant for lunch. The turn-of-the-century decor and formally clad waiters were pleasant and the food was always good. After lunch he would do a few errands, buy certain things he needed and then meet his chauffeur, who drove him to a large super-market on Insurgentes Avenue.

Bill would steer one shopping cart and his chauffeur would follow behind with another. Bill bought prodigiously — thirty artichokes, fifteen pounds of frozen shrimp, four dozen eggs and assorted delicacies he could not buy in Taxco. He always filled both carts and the money he paid at the check-out counter would have fed a large Mexican family for two months.

Then they would be back on the road and Bill would

watch his chauffeur's driving technique intently, hoping to catch him in a shifting error or a too closely hugged curve.

Bill Spratling was killed on August 7, 1967, as the result of an automobile accident on his final drive to Mexico City.

He awoke that morning at five o'clock as usual and later picked up his chauffeur in Iguala around five-thirty, then drove out of Iguala.

There is a straight stretch of road beyond Iguala and, as always, Bill took advantage of it to pick up speed. It was still dark so his headlights were on and suddenly they picked up a black shape looming in the road ahead. It had rained the night before and a tree had been uprooted by the rains and high winds. It had fallen across the highway, blocking it completely. It was five-forty-five.

Bill swerved in an effort to drive off the road and come to a safe halt, for he had not seen the fallen tree in time to stop. Instead, he crashed into another tree, head on. The impact broke the steering wheel and the shaft, against which Bill was thrown. It dislocated his hipbone, smashed part of his ribcage, and caused internal injuries that were not immediately apparent.

The chauffeur was badly shaken up but not otherwise injured. He quickly scrambled out of the car and began running back toward Iguala when a car approached him. The chauffeur flagged down the car, told them what had happened and went on toward Iguala. The automobile drove up to the scene of the accident, and when its driver saw that Bill was conscious, he offered to drive him into town to the nearest hospital. Bill refused and told the man to send for an ambulance.

The chauffeur had already called the ambulance and at six-twenty-five it finally arrived, forty minutes after the accident. Bill instructed the ambulance driver to take him directly to the doctor in Iguala who had treated him in the past.

In the doctor's office, he was X-rayed and was still conscious, complaining only of a pain in his chest. Antonio, Bill's majordomo and chef, had been called by the chauffeur and had driven to the doctor's office to be with his friend and employer. When he arrived, Bill was drinking a cup of coffee. Bill said to him: *"A ver si esta vez no me muero."* — We'll see if this time I won't die.

Just before he was taken from the doctor's office, Bill told Antonio to have his houseguest wakened and brought to the hospital. By coincidence, Bill's guest was the doctor he went to in the United States, Dr. John Bukowski of Houston, Texas. Dr. Bukowski had planned to drive to Mexico City with Bill, but Bill had awakened him shortly after five to tell him he did not have to get up that early. He could meet Bill later at the Monte Cassino. Now, at six-thirty, a servant woke Dr. Bukowski to tell him about the accident and that he was to go at once to either the doctor's office or the hospital. Dr. Bukowski went to the doctor's office and was shown the X-rays, but Bill had already been taken to the hospital. At the hospital, Dr. Bukowski was told that no "William Spratling" was registered there. Finally the doctor located Bill, still in the ambulance. But it was too late. Bill was dead of a heart attack he had suffered in the ambulance.

The rumors and reports that sifted through to me in Taxco were confusing, but one bleak fact was clear. Bill was dead. It was the kind of news that stuns the mind and numbs the senses. The reality of it was unacceptable to me. No part of me could believe that Bill had actually died. The report could not be true.

Dazed, I went slowly down to the Plaza Borda and hired a taxi to drive me to Bill's ranch, seven miles south. Often the drivers chat with their passengers, but now this one sat stiffly silent, indicating his own sorrow only with a sad shake of his head as I got into his car.

The ranch was surrounded by policemen from both Iguala and Taxco when I arrived. Bill's immensely valuable collection of pre-Columbian art had been placed immediately under guard. Dr. Bukowski had just returned from the hospital in Iguala and the mayor of Taxco, Jaime Castrejón, was already there, along with other officials from Taxco.

It was true then. I sat down in a chair on the patio and stared about me, only half hearing the muted murmuring of exchanged condolences and memories. Bill's wild, unkempt jungle that he had planted years before was unchanged; it looked unnaturally bright and green in the clear morning light. Around the massive table on the patio were scattered the frivolous plastic chairs that Bill had recently bought in Texas. The colors — cheerful green, red, blue, orange — held my attention. They should not be there.

Someone was speaking to me. After what seemed a long time, his words filtered through to me. It was Jaime Castrejón. He was telling me that Bill was to have a state funeral in Taxco, the city he had given his life to.

That was wrong. I stared at him for a moment, remembering. Only weeks before, Bill and I had been having lunch with Ted Wicks, whose house has a rolling panoramic view of all Taxco, with the cemetery at the foot of the hill. Ted had pointed to the little chapel in the cemetery and had made some remark that he would some day be buried there. "Good Lord," Bill exclaimed. "You can't really be serious. I'm glad I'm going to be cremated." We went on talking and Bill stated flatly that there would be no fuss about his funeral, for he did not intend to have any.

"No," I told Jaime Castrejón, "Bill wanted to be cremated. He told me so."

Jaime was very gentle as he explained to me that all of the people of Taxco would want to be able to pay their final homage to their benefactor. Bill had left all his pre-Columbian art to the city of Taxco to be housed in a museum that was going to be built. A funeral for Bill was inevitable.

I nodded quietly. William Spratling was Taxco's living legend and would have to be interred as such. Bill was my younger brother, my dearest friend. My own funeral service for Bill would be silent and in my mind — the lingering, poignant memories of him.

Tony Reyes, the owner of the Cantarranas nightclub in Taxco, and Pedro Perras, who has a large silver shop, did all the paper work that was necessary before Bill's body was released by the Iguala police into their care. He was brought back to the ranch briefly and then someone drove me in a long, mournful procession back to Taxco. As we drove into town the thought passed fleetingly through my mind that this was the first time Bill had been in Taxco in the daytime in over ten years.

Bill's body was placed in an expensive gray metal coffin and he lay "in state" in the main room on the top floor of the *Presidencia*, which is the city hall of Taxco. There, Elias Alvarado made three death masks of Bill, one of which was later cast into bronze at my request. Hundreds and hundreds of people filed by the open casket for their last look and left flowers.

At six o'clock that evening, the casket was closed, and Bill's friends, following the Mexican custom, took turns standing by the casket in a vigil throughout the night. Three men at a time stood alongside the casket for a length of time, then were replaced by three more. At midnight, the lights were turned down but the vigil continued.

The funeral was to be held at three o'clock the next afternoon, and early the next morning flowers began to appear along the wrought-iron grillwork of the gate to the courtyard of Santa Prisca. I could not understand it. Bill was no Catholic, had no religion at all, but somehow they were awarding him a High Mass in the Catholic Church.

The mayor had proclaimed two official days of mourning and all the shops were closed when I went down to the plaza to attend the funeral service at Santa Prisca. The laurel trees that circled the plaza had been planted from clippings from the trees at Bill's ranch. Now I saw, for the second time in my life, the little black bugs moving slowly toward the church, the little old ladies in black *rebozos* who had painfully left their reclusion to go to the funeral of Don Guillermo, just as they had gone to pray when the Virgin had fallen.

The town seemed to be in a state of shock. People stood around in little groups, not talking, just standing together as if taking comfort in the mere presence of others.

Large black bows of ribbon were hung on all the doors of the shops and houses. I glanced up at the balustrade of the Bar Paco, where puzzled, subdued tourists were drinking. Three huge black bows hung there. I had noticed, on my way to the Plaza, that the street sign for the Calle de Guillermo Spratling had been draped in black. In front of the church, there were great banks of flowers. Enormous heavy wheels of flowers, five feet tall, had been propped up against the iron fence. Each one had a ribbon that bore the name of the person who had sent it. There was a bank of flowers along the east side of the church at least a hundred feet long.

At three-forty-five, John L. Brown, the cultural attaché of the U.S. Embassy in Mexico City, emerged from the *Presidencia*, followed by Jaime Castrejón, Antonio Castillo and several other old friends of Bill's. They were followed by ten men — all Bill's silversmiths — who bore the gray casket in a slow procession to the Santa Prisca Basilica. They placed the casket in front of the altar, on the steps.

By bad luck, the day before had been the day of Padre Jesus. His statue had been stuck up behind the altar, about six feet tall, dressed in white cheesecloth and wearing a crown of spiky tin thorns. Near him, the statue of the Virgin had been placed. It all seemed so wrong for Bill's funeral.

It was a dull, overcast day, but the sun came out just at the right moment. Through the windows over the pulpit, the gold light slanted, illuminating the casket. Bill would have thought it corny.

At four-ten the Mass began, and later the priest was droning on about the life everlasting and the virtues of being a good Catholic. It struck me, incongruously, that at least Bill did not have to hear all this. Outside, loudspeakers blared the Mass to the throngs that jammed the plaza, until some urchin pulled the wires. Someone tried to repair the speakers, but only an earsplitting screech of static resulted.

A few minutes before five o'clock, about thirty men picked up the great wheels of flowers and started the funeral march from Santa Prisca to the cemetery. They were followed by the coffin, still borne aloft by his silversmiths. Then came the crowds of black-clad mourners, ten abreast. It took forty-five minutes for the procession to go down the steep cobblestone hill to the cemetery. There were at least six hundred people on foot, followed by an equal number in cars, plumbers' trucks and station wagons. All over Taxco, people stood on rooftops, craning for a last glimpse of Don Guillermo.

At the cemetery, Bill's coffin was lowered into a cement-lined grave. John L. Brown delivered a speech in Spanish, as did Jaime Castrejón and a woman judge. Someone from a local radio station recorded it all on a portable tape recorder. Newspaper photographers were literally hanging from nearby tombs.

By six-fifteen, it was all over and the crowds dispersed slowly, as if reluctant to go.

I was alone in my house and I sat quietly, not thinking, simply aware of a terrible emptiness in my life.

Months later, I went out to Bill's ranch where his silver was still being sold to tourists who were flocking to the scene to buy what they could of Bill's last designs. I went around to the living quarters, an area never invaded by curious tourists.

Armed guards still stood at the entrance to the small museum Bill had built to house his pre-Columbian collection. Everything was labeled and catalogued by the government except a huge pre-Columbian stone egg in the garden. Bill had once told me it was one of his most valuable possessions. Evidently the labelers had mistaken it for merely a big stone.

On the flagstones of the patio, the frivolous swivel chairs were gathering dust and the plastic was cracking from the humidity.

It was strange, I thought. I miss Bill Spratling so very much more than I ever missed Sherwood Anderson.

 nineteen

The clouds are intimate with the mountains in Taxco, resting on their tops, drifting in the ravines, hovering, ragging, curling up in the crevices. I wake early in the morning to watch the start of the new day, to chart its predictable course. If the clouds are creeping in from the north, the rains will come, for all our bad weather comes from Mexico City, they say, while all the good comes from the *tierra caliente* in the south.

The bells of Santa Prisca have already begun, at five-thirty, to summon the faithful to church and to reprimand the faithless for staying at home. The priests get together and say, "This is a good time for it to be five-thirty," and the bells are rung, setting the time standard for the day. Those with clocks set them according to the bells, and if some tourists are startled to hear the bells ringing for noon at eleven-fifty or twelve-thirteen, it is of little import. For those who live in Taxco, it is noon when the noon bells ring. And that is as it should be, for the exact time means little in Taxco, where no planes land on a tightly regimented schedule and no time clocks tick their moneyed minutes. If one wishes to take a bus out of this city, one has only to call the bus station to find out what time *they* have.

There are two bell towers and two bells, and the effect is that of two bells ringing, but it is an illusion. Actually there are two clappers inside a single bell, being activated by two young boys who have had to learn the solemnity of their task. They must not ring at random, for there is a meaningful pattern to the ceremony.

Within seconds after the bells of Santa Prisca have sounded, there is the distant clanging of the bells of the *ex-convento*, which seems almost in competition with the bells of the bigger church. Then the other seven churches begin to ring their bells, each with an individual tone and pattern. The bells of Santa Prisca are the loudest and most impressive, though not up to the standard of European bells. The other bells in town have tones that range from leaden to tinny. One of them sounds like a large spoon being rattled in a tin pail.

The clouds are drifting in from the *tierra caliente*. It will be a good day. From my terrace I survey all of Taxco and it is a pleasant sight. It has been decreed by the government that Taxco should remain in appearance as it is now. All improvements must be made on the interior of the houses, for there must be no shiny outside plumbing to flash in the sunlight and there must be no angled, modernistic structure to stand out from all the rest. No one may paint houses or walls any color but pink or brown and only the church and state dare defy this decree. In all of Taxco, only the public school and the walls of the house of the priests are green.

I am a part of this town. I have lived with its legends and have taken part in its rituals, some of which are singular. At one time of the year, all the young girls are allowed to go out without chaperones, though no one talks of this or plans for it. On a certain special day, all the young girls in Taxco leave their houses early in the morning, before the sun is up, to go up into the hills. All the young men of Taxco also leave their houses to go up into the hills, but they take a different route than the girls. At a set time, they meet and talk to each other across the hills for a time, and then the two groups combine to hunt for *humiles* to place in the tin cup that each one carries. *Humiles* are a dubious delicacy — small bugs that smell rather like bedbugs. They are pickled in vinegar and salt and pepper and eaten with apparently great relish. Some say this clandestine rendezvous in the hills is the source of sporadic population explosions, but I have always doubted that. The meeting is too pure in concept, too traditional in tone. The boys and girls simply get together in the mountains to hunt *humiles* and to later eat them like candy.

On the Day of the Virgin of Guadalupe, the entire town takes part in the celebration. To begin with, everyone who has done anything he is even slightly remorseful about sends an offering to the church. This is usually in the form of a great many candles on a string or a bouquet of flowers. The Church of the Virgin of Guadalupe is high up in the mountains, in the uppermost part of Taxco to which tourists seldom venture, simply because the climb is so arduous. Down in the plaza a band is playing, more sedately than usual because they do not wish to disturb the Virgin.

The Virgin has been shut up in the church with San Miguel for an entire night and day. Very late on the night before, the statue of St. Michael, or San Miguel, was taken from his church in lower Taxco and was very secretly brought up to visit the Virgin of Guadalupe in her church. He is left to spend the night and day with the Virgin. No one in Taxco seems to think this is at all strange except me.

When it is dark on the Day of the Virgin, San Miguel is deemed to have had enough time alone with her. The band starts moving out of the Plaza Borda, up toward the church of the Virgin. They are still playing and are followed by a long procession consisting of everyone in town, all with lighted candles, perhaps to warn the Virgin they are coming. The music of the band is a bit strained before they reach the church, but they go on making whatever noise they can.

It is a lovely sight, these hundreds of lighted candles bobbing and weaving as the procession winds its way through the narrow, twisting streets of Taxco. At the church, the statue of San Miguel has been spirited out of public sight. All the candles are placed before the Virgin, who, it is true, has a faint smile on her lips, a Mass is held, and the people slowly slip away into the night.

Very early in the morning, before anyone is awake to watch, the statue of San Miguel is sneaked back down the hill to his own church. This, too, is a tradition that everyone knows about but no one speaks about. I have seen the statue of San Miguel as it is carried down the hill. He is covered over with a cloak as he is carted down the hills, through the back streets and alleys and into the back door of his church.

Taxco has changed considerably since first I saw it, a pink and brown mosaic cupped into the side of a mountain. Many new houses have been built, crowded next to and on top of the other houses. The ravine that had been a jungle, separating Bill Spratling's spartan digs from Natalie Scott's salon, is now completely filled with houses. From Bill Spratling's first factory, Las Delicias, have come a great many silver factories by a form of fission, the single cell cleaving into many cells.

The tourists, too, have changed. At one time people came to Taxco looking for a quiet retreat in which to write or paint. Others came looking for adventure and passed through Taxco in their quest for it. They were a sprightly lot, eager to milk from life all the fine nectar, quick to savor the taste of it. The people who come to Taxco now are, perhaps, more ordinary, for it is no longer an epic journey. They are nice people but, with a few delightful exceptions, lack the style and flair of those who came before them.

And I have changed. I lead a quiet life, with my old friends and employees coming each day to sit in my back room and sew and chat, exchanging the changing gossip of the town. They have grown old with me and the daughters of their daughters now work at their side.

At the age of eighty-four, I no longer go to many parties; it is too difficult to follow the line of one conversation against a background medley of many conversations. I prefer a good book, and quite often the good books of old friends. It is more difficult for me to navigate the hills of Taxco, but I manage by moving more slowly. Someone has suggested that a golf cart might be modified so that it could manage the slopes, but the image of myself steering a canvas-topped, gaily colored golf cart through Taxco is more comic than practical.

It is a Saturday and the day that began well, with clouds coming from the *tierra caliente*, has progressed nicely. The sun has dissipated the wispy clouds and the sky is a bright, glowing blue. It is a good day to go to the *mercado* to shop.

I take the back way to the *mercado*, for there are short stretches of sidewalks set into the cobblestones, and the slopes are longer and less steep. The *mercado* is a long way down, far below the church of Santa Prisca, but I am in no hurry. Once there, I stop at the small shop at which I buy the material for my embroideresses. I inquire about the clerk's sister, who has had an operation. She is fine, better than last week, I am told. I order the materials which will be sent up later, and look over a new stock which arrived yesterday. I move through the *mercado*, stopping to ask about a pair of shoes at the cobbler's, checking the price of meat at the butcher's. Then I return, going the front way, through the Plaza Borda and up the Calle de Guillermo Spratling to my house.

311

At the crossing of one narrow lane with another, even narrower lane, there is a blockade of six enormous pigs being unsuccessfully herded by a small boy. It is an impasse. The pigs will not move past the corner. I cannot. The small boy looks helplessly at me and shrugs. The pigs mill about, jostling and grunting. I know about pigs. I take hold of the rope attached to the first pig's nose ring and give a strong yank in the direction in which he is supposed to be moving. He moves. The pigs pour through the lane as if they have been squirted through a tube. I go on.

"*Gracias, Señora,*" the small boy calls, chasing after his pigs.

It is late afternoon when the embroideresses leave, after having collected their wages. I sit out on my small patio, watching the black puffs of skyrockets being sent up to celebrate some occasion. I can recall sitting in the Bar Paco with Bill Spratling and the owner of the silver mines outside Taxco. Each time a skyrocket exploded, with an enormous bang, he would mutter, "There goes more of our dynamite." Finally I asked him why he did not lock up his precious dynamite if he did not want the workers to use it. "They'd strike," he said. "They'd never work if they couldn't use the dynamite."

The skyrockets that are exploding now seem more powerful than most. Even the ordinary ones have three times the amount of explosives than comparable ones in the United States. Somewhere in Taxco, there must be a heady celebration under way.

The light fades from the sky slowly, subtly changing the colors of the town and deepening the shadows. My two Siamese cats are lying peacefully on the ledge of the patio. They have a curious facility for arranging themselves in patterns that are pleasing to the eye, as if each cat were aware of the pose of the other and were adapting to it to achieve an aesthetic effect. I have never found them in repose when they were not gracefully arranged.

It is dark now and the tailor in the little shop a few yards down the street is using his steam presser. A single yellow light is over his doorway and the presser sends out luminous clouds of lemon-colored steam into the night. In the Plaza Borda, the Saturday night band is tuning up and soon it is in full swing. The sound is gentled by the distance and not unpleasant. I listen to it for a long time.

Late that night, while I am listening to the band playing and the people chattering down on the plaza, there is an electrical failure. All the lights in Taxco go out at once and immediately I can hear the delighted screams of girls and boys down in the plaza. In the darkened bowl of Taxco, I can see the gradual flickering of more and more candles, and the distant cries for still more: *"Velas!"* The youths of the town are having a hilarious time in the dark plaza.

Then the lights go on again, all together, just as they had gone out. It gives the effect of a mammoth Christmas tree being illuminated for a ceremonious occasion. The town sighs collectively, but it is not a sigh of relief. The brief plunge into darkness has harmed no one. To the contrary, new friendships have been formed, new romances have flared up. It was a change in routine and that is always a delight in a small town.

I sit quietly in the dark night, along with the past. Memories linger with me, but do not crowd. It is the good times that I recall most vividly: the sharp tang of a Michigan winter; the sequestered world of books in a shop at Lord and Taylor's; a lovely blue lake near Reno and a lover who wore blue shirts; the chiaroscuro effect of New Orleans with its intense hot sunlight and darkened, twisting alleys and cool, dim bars; the heady air of a Paris winter; the collective good will of the housebuilders of Ripshin; the bustling clatter of linotype machines; and a cat who loved a chicken, not wisely, but too well.

The people, too, are with me still: the solemn set to Bill Faulkner's face as he spun outrageous lies about his flamboyant past; the pool-dark look of Sherwood's eyes as he told me of his dreams and private anguishes; the thrust-jawed angularity of Bill Spratling's face during so many conversations over so many years; and many more, the companions of my reflective moods.

The band music in the plaza has stopped and the people have all gone to their homes. Slowly the lights around the town go out and the still hours of the night settle over Taxco peacefully.

The Bryant Library
Roslyn, New York
Telephone: MA 1-2240